First World War
and Army of Occupation
War Diary
France, Belgium and Germany

55 DIVISION
166 Infantry Brigade,
Brigade Machine Gun Company
8 May 1916 - 28 February 1918

WO95/2930/2

The Naval & Military Press Ltd
www.nmarchive.com
Published in association with The National Archives

Published by

The Naval & Military Press Ltd

Unit 10 Ridgewood Industrial Park,
Uckfield, East Sussex,
TN22 5QE England
Tel: +44 (0) 1825 749494

www.naval-military-press.com
www.nmarchive.com

Contents

Document type	Place/Title	Date From	Date To
Heading	WO95/2930/2 166 Infantry Bde Brigade Machine Gun Coy May 1916-Feb 1918		
Heading	55th Division 166th Infy Bde 166th Machine Gun Coy May 1916-Feb 1918		
War Diary		08/05/1916	31/05/1916
Heading	War Diary Of 166th Inf Brigade Machine Gun Coy From June 1st 1916 To June 30th 1916 Vol 4		
War Diary	Grosville	01/06/1916	30/06/1916
Heading	166th Brigade 55th Division 166th Brigade Machine Gun Company July 1916		
Heading	War Diary Of 166th Machine Gun Company For July 1916 Vol 5		
War Diary	Grosville	01/07/1916	08/07/1916
War Diary	Beaumetz	11/07/1916	11/07/1916
War Diary	Dainville	12/07/1916	16/07/1916
War Diary	Gouy	17/07/1916	17/07/1916
War Diary	Grand Rullecourt	18/07/1916	18/07/1916
War Diary	Lucheux	20/07/1916	20/07/1916
War Diary	Le Meillard	21/07/1916	21/07/1916
War Diary	Houdencourt	22/07/1916	24/07/1916
War Diary	Ville Sur Ancre	25/07/1916	25/07/1916
War Diary	Meaulte	27/07/1916	31/07/1916
Heading	166th Brigade 55th Division 166th Brigade Machine Gun Company August 1916		
Heading	War Diary Of The 166th Bde M.G. Coy For The Period 1st August To 31st August 1916 Vol 6		
War Diary	Mansell Copse	01/08/1916	19/08/1916
War Diary	Saucourt	20/08/1916	31/08/1916
Miscellaneous	Report On Operations	11/08/1916	11/08/1916
Heading	166th Machine Gun Company War Diary For September 1916 Vol 7		
War Diary	Meaulte	01/09/1916	29/09/1916
Miscellaneous	Report On Operations	10/09/1916	10/09/1916
Heading	War Diary Of 166th Machine Gun Company For October 1916 Vol 8		
War Diary	Ribemont	30/09/1916	17/10/1916
War Diary	Ypres	18/10/1916	31/10/1916
Heading	War Diary For Month Of November 1916 Of 166th Machine Gun Company Vol 9		
War Diary	Ypres	02/11/1916	18/11/1916
War Diary	Brandhoek	19/11/1916	27/11/1916
War Diary	Ypres	15/11/1916	18/11/1916
War Diary	Brandhoek	19/11/1916	29/11/1916
Heading	War Diary Of 166th Machine Gun Coy For Period December 1st-31st 1916 Vol 10		
War Diary	Canal Bank Ypres	01/12/1916	17/12/1916
War Diary	Brandhoek	18/12/1916	26/12/1916
War Diary	Canal Bank Ypres	27/12/1916	30/12/1916
Heading	War Diary Of The 166th M.G. Coy For The Period 1/1/17 To 31/1/17 Vol XI		

War Diary	Canal Bank Ypres	01/01/1917	16/01/1917
War Diary	Bollezeele	17/01/1917	31/01/1917
Heading	War Diary Of 166th M.G. Coy For The Period 1st To 28th February 1917 Vol 12		
War Diary	Bollezeele	01/02/1917	17/02/1917
War Diary	Canal Bank Ypres	18/02/1917	28/02/1917
Heading	War Diary Of The 166th M.G. Coy For The Period 1st To 31st March 1917 Vol 13		
War Diary	Branhoek	28/02/1917	28/03/1917
Heading	War Diary Of 166th Machine Gun Coy For The Period April 1st To 30th 1917 Vol 14		
War Diary	Brandhoek	01/04/1917	07/04/1917
War Diary	Ypres	16/04/1917	30/04/1917
Heading	War Diary Of 166 M.G. Coy For The Period May 1st-31st 1917 Vol 15		
War Diary	Ypres	01/05/1917	12/05/1917
War Diary	St. Janter Biezen	13/05/1917	19/05/1917
War Diary	Ypres	20/05/1917	31/05/1917
Heading	War Diary Of 166th M.G. Coy For The Period June 1st To June 30th 1917 Vol 16		
War Diary	Ypres	01/06/1917	14/06/1917
War Diary	Potijze	14/06/1917	22/06/1917
War Diary	Quelmes	23/06/1917	30/06/1917
Heading	War Diary Of The 166th M.G. Coy For The Period 1st July To 31st July 1917 Vol 17		
War Diary	Quelmes	01/07/1917	20/07/1917
War Diary	Ypres	20/07/1917	30/07/1917
War Diary	Wieltje	31/07/1917	31/07/1917
Heading	War Diary Of 166th M.G. Co For Period 1st To 31st August 1917 Vol 18		
War Diary	Wieltje	01/08/1917	19/08/1917
War Diary	Nordausque	25/08/1917	31/08/1917
Heading	War Diary Of 166th M.G. Coy For Period 1/9/17-30/9/17 Vol 19		
War Diary	Nordausque	02/09/1917	19/09/1917
War Diary	St Jean	19/09/1917	22/09/1917
War Diary	Ypres	22/09/1917	30/09/1917
Heading	War Diary Of The 166th M.G. Coy For The Period 1st To 31st October 1917 Vol 20		
War Diary	In The Field	01/10/1917	31/10/1917
Heading	War Diary Of The 166th M.G. Co For The Period 1st To 30th November 1917 Vol 21		
War Diary	In The Field France Sheet 57. E SE 4	01/11/1917	07/11/1917
War Diary	In The Field	08/11/1917	30/11/1917
Heading	War Diary Of The 166th Machine Gun Coy For The Period 1st To 31st December 1917 Vol 22		
War Diary	In The Field Epehy	03/12/1917	14/12/1917
War Diary	In The Field	15/12/1917	31/12/1917
Heading	War Diary Of The 166th M.G. Coy For The Period 1st To 31st January 1918 Vol 23		
War Diary	Petigny	01/01/1918	31/01/1918
Heading	War Diary Of The 166th M.G. Coy For The Period 1st To 28th Febry 1918 Vol 24		
War Diary	Petigny	01/02/1918	14/02/1918
War Diary	In The Field	24/02/1918	28/02/1918

WO 95/2930/2

166 INFANTRY BDE

BRIGADE MACHINE GUN COY

MAY 1916 - FEB 1918

55TH DIVISION

166TH INFY BDE

166TH MACHINE GUN COY.

MAY 1916-FEB 1918

Instructions regarding War Diaries and Intelligence Summaries are contained in F. S. Regs., Part II, and the Staff Manual respectively. Title Pages will be prepared in manuscript.

WAR DIARY
or
~~INTELLIGENCE SUMMARY~~
(Erase heading not required).

Army Form C. 2118. 53

166 Bde M G Coy

Vol 3

Place	Date	Hour	Summary of Events and Information	Remarks and references to Appendices
	8/5/16		Indirect fire on roads in FICHEUX + neighbouring trenches + tracks, on trench + tracks at 36 a. 5.3. All quiet.	REF TRENCH MAP FICHEUX 51C. SE. + 51 B. SW (Parts of) Edition 2. B! 1/10.000.
	9/5/16		Indirect fire on sunken road at R 35 D. 10. 96. QUARRY at BLAIREVILLE + sunken road + trench at M 35 d 1.6. All quiet.	
	10/5/16		Indirect fire on QUARRY in BLAIREVILLE WOOD + on roads in FICHEUX + neighbouring trenches. All quiet.	
	11/5/16		No 1 Section relieved No 4 in FRONT LINE. No 4 relieved No 2 in PETIT CHATEAU + WAILLY KEEP. No 2 relieved No 1 in MILL POST + TERRITORIAL LINE. Indirect fire on BLAIREVILLE QUARRY. All quiet.	
	12/5/16		Indirect fire on trench + tracks at R 36 a 5 3, on tracks + trenches at M 25 b 65. 40. + on trenches at M 25 d. 10. 60. All quiet	
	13/5/16		Indirect fire on roads in FICHEUX VILLAGE + neighbouring trenches. All quiet.	
	14/5/16		Company relieved by 164th + 166th Brigade M G Coys, the former taking over two left positions in FRONT LINE, LEFT PETIT CHATEAU + LEFT WAILLY KEEP positions + the latter two right positions in FRONT LINE, RIGHT MILL POST + LEFT WAILLY KEEP positions. No 3 Section attached to 166th Brigade M G Coy [illegible] relieved by Third Coy. Company proceeded to GOUY.	
	15/5/16		Company arrived at GOUY 1-0 am.	

H M Bain Capt
for O/C 165th. Brigade,
M/G. Coy.

BSD - B. M351 22/11. 12/15. 5000.

Instructions regarding War Diaries and Intelligence Summaries are contained in F. S. Regs., Part II, and the Staff Manual respectively. Title Pages will be prepared in manuscript.

WAR DIARY

or

~~INTELLIGENCE SUMMARY~~

(Erase heading not required).

Army Form C. 2118.

Place	Date	Hour	Summary of Events and Information	Remarks and references to Appendices
	16/5/16 to 29/5/16		Training at GOUY	REF. 1 TRENCH MAP. FICHEUX 51c S.E. 4 51b S.W. (Parts of) Edition 2. B. 1. 10.000
	30/5/16		Company left GOUY 7-30 pm. & took up positions as follows:- No 3 Section in FRONT LINE, No 1 PETIT CHATEAU, & WAILLY KEEP, No 4 at MILL-POST & TERRITORIAL LINE No 2 in reserve at LE FERMONT. Indirect fire carried out by 166th Bgde M/G Coy on FICHEUX & neighbouring trenches & tracks.	
	31/5/16		New position at WAILLY (R 23. a 3 6.) taken over by team of No 2 section. Indirect fire carried out on FICHEUX & neighbouring trenches & tracks. BLAIRSVILLE QUARRY, sunken road at R. 35. b 0.0., road & tracks & trenches at R. 36. a 5.3 & sunken road & trenches at M. 25 d. 1. 6.	

H. McCann Capt
for O/C 165th. Brigade, M/G. Coy.

BSD - B. M351 22/11. 12/15 5000.

558

CONFIDENTIAL

Vol 4

WAR DIARY

of

166th Inf. Brigade Machine Gun Coy.

from June 1st 1916 to June 30th 1916.

Army Form C. 2118

Instructions regarding War Diaries and Intelligence Summaries are contained in F. S. Regs., Part II. and the Staff Manual respectively. Title Pages will be prepared in manuscript.

WAR DIARY
or
INTELLIGENCE SUMMARY
(Erase heading not required.)

Place	Date	Hour	Summary of Events and Information	Remarks and references to Appendices
GROSVILLE	June 1.		Strength of Unit. 8 offs. 156 O.R. 53 horses.	
	2	9.15 PM	Enemy wiring party located at X.2C.2.7. and dispersed by M. G. and LEWIS Gun fire. (MAP. REF. TRENCH MAP. FICHEUX, 26. 1/10,000).	
	4	12.30 AM	Artillery very active on both sides	
	5		4 officers 44 other ranks attached for instruction.	
	6		Stakes for barbed wire put out at X.2.d.5.3. (Trench MAP FICHEUX.2.6.) by enemy	
	9		1 O.R. reinforcement from M. G. corps.	
	10	1.15 AM	Enemy working party located on barbed wire left of LES 3 MAISONS (Trench Map FICHEUX 26.) and dispersed by M. G. fire.	
	11	10.30 PM	Enemy working party located on barbed wire at X.3.a.5.5½. (Trench Map FICHEUX). Fire was directed on this point, but result was not observed.	KAW
	13		Barbed wire observed to have been put out at X.26.10.5. (Trench MAP. FICHEUX) by enemy. Barbed wire very thick at this point.	
	15	4 PM	Enemy sent a few shells near new emplacement at R.32.C.7.4. (Trench Map FICHEUX).	
	16		Reinforced by 1 officer and 1 other rank (saddler)	
	18		Aeroplanes active on both sides. Enemy planes driven off by our own.	
	21		Enemy made a new Communication Trench from about X.2.d.8.6. to X.2.d.5.8. (Trench Map FICHEUX). A lot of wire has been put along side of road from X.2.d.5.0 to X.2.d.8.6 (Trench Map FICHEUX).	

1875 Wt. W593/826 1,000,000 4/15 J.B.C. & A. A.D.S.S./Forms/C. 2118.

Instructions regarding War Diaries and Intelligence Summaries are contained in F. S. Regs., Part II. and the Staff Manual respectively. Title Pages will be prepared in manuscript.

WAR DIARY
or
INTELLIGENCE SUMMARY
(Erase heading not required.)

Army Form C. 2118

Place	Date	Hour	Summary of Events and Information	Remarks and references to Appendices
GROSVILLE	June 23	12 MIDN.	Enemy wiring party located immediately in front of BLOCKHOUSE in X.2.b. (Trench Map FICHEUX).	
	24		Enemy M.G's active during night.	
	25		Enemy M.G's active during night.	
	26/27		During night artillery bombarded FICHEUX, RANSART and BLAIRVILLE. Machine Guns operated in conjunction with artillery and fired into these villages.	
	27/28		During the night fire was directed on villages in conjunction with artillery.	
	28		An operation in the form of a raid on the enemy's trenches was arranged and attempted at 5. P.m. The raiding party was to enter enemy sap at X.3.b.45.85. (Trench Map FICHEUX 51C. S.E. & 51B. S.W. part of). Gas was used. The gas cloud barely touched the enemy's sap but seemed to pass away to the left of it (N.E.). A party of about 15 GERMANS were seen on the parapet or parados at X.3.b.9.8 (Trench Map FICHEUX), and fire was directed on them, but result could not be observed. A few enemy rifles opened fire after the gas cloud had passed. The enemy sent very few big shells over & his artillery did not put up anything in the form of a barrage & gave one the impression	JBW

Army Form C. 2118

Instructions regarding War Diaries and Intelligence Summaries are contained in F. S. Regs., Part II. and the Staff Manual respectively. Title Pages will be prepared in manuscript.

WAR DIARY
or
INTELLIGENCE SUMMARY
(Erase heading not required.)

Place	Date	Hour	Summary of Events and Information	Remarks and references to Appendices
			that he had not many guns firing. Cease fire was ordered at 5 35 P.m. 10,000 rounds S.A.A. were expended. Casualties nil.	JHW
	29/30		Machine Gun fire was kept up on villages of BLAIREVILLE & RANSART in conjunction with artillery.	

1875 Wt. W593/826 1,000,000 4/15 J.B.C. & A. A.D.S.S./Forms/C. 2118.

166th Brigade.

55th Division.

166th BRIGADE MACHINE GUN COMPANY

JULY 1 9 1 6

~~Confidential~~

Vol 5

War Diary

of

166th Machine Gun Company

for

July 1916.

Instructions regarding War Diaries and Intelligence Summaries are contained in F. S. Regs., Part II. and the Staff Manual respectively. Title Pages will be prepared in manuscript.

WAR DIARY
or
INTELLIGENCE SUMMARY
(Erase heading not required.)

Army Form C. 2118

Place	Date	Hour	Summary of Events and Information	Remarks and references to Appendices
GROSVILLE	July 1st		Strength of Unit-- 9 Officers, 158 O.R.s (4 Offs, 43 O.R. attch. for instruction) 54 horses.	
			Enemy M.G. located in X 2 b behind BLOCKHOUSE (FICHEUX Trench Map)	
		6-30 a.m.	Enemy aeroplane dropped bomb in WILLOWS support trenches.	
			Fire was directed on village of RANSART during night of 30/1st. ~~Enemy~~	
			During the night of 1/2nd enemy used searchlights.	
		9-0 - 10-0 p.m.	Enemy aeroplanes very active	
	2nd	10-30 - 11-30 p.m.	Enemy working party in front of BLOCKHOUSE was dispersed by artillery fire.	
			Fire was directed into RANSART.	
	3rd	1-50 p.m.	Enemy observation balloon brought down in flames by one of our aeroplanes.	
	4th		=1 Officer reinforcement -- 2nd Lt Davey. M.G.Corps.	
		1-0 - 2-0 a.m.	Transport heard behind RANSART ~~between~~	
			One of our Gun emplacements (LANDAFFE SUPPORT) blown in by shell fire, tripod smashed and ammunition boxes damaged.	
	5th.		Enemy shelled support trenches during afternoon.	
	6th		Copper bullet picked up in trench after striking sand-bag.	
	9th		2 Horses drawn from Mobile Vet.	
	8th		2 of our aeroplanes brought down by enemy. One in enemy's lines at 4-45 p.m. and one behind our own lines about 7-0 p.m.	
BEAUMETZ	11th		Company relieved by 139th Bde: M.G.Coy and moved to BEAUMETZ.	
DAINVILLE	12th	7-0 p.m.	Company move to DAINVILLE and take over position from 164th Bde:M.G.Coy. at AGNY. Headquarters at DAINVILLE.	
	14th		Five Machine Guns co-operated with Artillery between 3-0 a.m. and 4-0 a.m. Fire was directed on BEAURAINS and roads and tracks in rear of enemy front line system. Enemy retaliated and shelled our Gun emplacements. One shell dropped on one of the emplacements and buried the gun.	
		11-15 p.m.	Airship appeared over DAINVILLE about 11-15 p.m.	
	16th		32nd Bde: M.G.Coy arrive at DAINVILLE to relieve 166th Bde: M.G.Coy.	
GOUY	17th		32nd Bde: M.G.Coy relieved this company which proceeded to GOUY.	
GRAND RULLECOURT	18th	7-15 p.m.	Company left GOUY and moved to GRAND RULLECOURT.	
LUCHEUX	20th	6-30 a.m.	Company left GRAND RULLECOURT ~~at 6-30~~ and proceeded to LUCHEUX.	

1875 Wt. W593/826 1,000,000 4/15 J.B.C. & A. A.D.S.S./Forms/C. 2118.

Instructions regarding War Diaries and Intelligence Summaries are contained in F. S. Regs., Part II. and the Staff Manual respectively. Title pages will be prepared in manuscript.

WAR DIARY
or
INTELLIGENCE SUMMARY.
(Erase heading not required.)

Army Form C. 2118.

Place	Date	Hour	Summary of Events and Information	Remarks and references to Appendices
	1916 July			
LE MEILLARD	21st	6-30am	Company left LUCHEUX & proceeded to LE MEILLARD (Map – LENS 11)	
HOUDENCOURT	22nd	6-30am	″ ″ LE MEILLARD. ″ ″ HOUDENCOURT (″ ″)	
″	24th	6-30am	Company Transport left HOUDENCOURT & proceeded to COISY. (″ ″)	
VILLE SUR ANCRE	25th	6-15am	Company Transport left COISY & proceeded to VILLE SUR ANCRE (Map – France 57c)	
″	″	4-15am	Company left HOUDENCOURT & proceeded to CANDAS where they entrained at 11-30 a.m.	
″		5.0pm	Company arrived at MERICOURT having travelled from CANDAS via FLIXECOURT & AMIENS.	
″		6-0pm	Company marched from MERICOURT to VILLE-SUR-ANCRE.	
MEAULTE	27th	4-50pm	″ ″ ″ VILLE SUR ANCRE to SANDPITS – S.E. of MEAULTE where they bivouaced near the other battalions in the brigade.	
″	28th		During the afternoon 14 observation balloons could be seen in the Allies lines. ″ the evening 18 ″ ″ ″ ″ ″ ″ ″ ″. During the night of 28/29th a terrific bombardment could be heard.	
″	29th			
″	30th	10am	Company move to MENSALL COPSE in bivouacs. Enemy aeroplane came over and dropped several bombs.	
	31st			

T.134. Wt. W708–776. 500000. 4/15. Sir J. C. & S.

166th Brigade.
55th Division.

166th BRIGADE MACHINE GUN COMPANY

AUGUST 1 9 1 6

166 M.G.Co
Vol. 6

War Diary

of the

166th Bde. M.G. Coy

for the period

1st August to 31st August

1916.

Instructions regarding War Diaries and Intelligence Summaries are contained in F. S. Regs., Part II. and the Staff Manual respectively. Title pages will be prepared in manuscript.

WAR DIARY
or
INTELLIGENCE SUMMARY.
(Erase heading not required.)

Army Form C. 2118.

Place	Date	Hour	Summary of Events and Information	Remarks and references to Appendices
MANSELL COPSE	Aug. 1	6.30am.	Company move to reserve trenches E. of CARNOY.	
	2		Officers visited front line E. of TRONES WOOD.	
	6		COMPANY move into bivouacs nr. MANSELL COPSE.	
	8	7PM.	COMPANY move into front line	
	9		Report on operations attached	
	10		Company relieved by 72nd M.G. Coy. and move into Bivouacs	
	12		Company move into reserve trenches E. of CARNOY. Operation for 12th 13th & 14th attached on separate sheet.	
	14		Company relieved by 76th M.G. Coy. and 9th M.G. Coy	
	15	4PM.	Company move into billets at MEAULTE.	
	16	6PM.	Company inspected by G.O.C. 55th Division.	
	17	4PM.	Company transport move via AMIENS, & ABBEVILLE to SAUCOURT	
	19	8.30am.	Company move by train to MARTAINVILLE and marched from there to billets at SAUCOURT.	

T.134. Wt. W708–776. 500000. 4/15. Sir J. C. & S.

Instructions regarding War Diaries and Intelligence Summaries are contained in F. S. Regs., Part II. and the Staff Manual respectively. Title pages will be prepared in manuscript.

WAR DIARY
or
INTELLIGENCE SUMMARY.
(Erase heading not required.)

Army Form C. 2118.

Place	Date	Hour	Summary of Events and Information	Remarks and references to Appendices
SAUCOURT	20th to 28th		Company training	[illegible]
	28th	2.30PM.	Transport move to bivouac 2 miles W. of ALBERT via AMIENS.	
	29th	3 PM.	Company move to BOENCOURT	
	30th	3am	Company move to PONT REMY and entrain for MERICOURT, and afterwards march to bivouac 2 miles W. of ALBERT.	
	31st	2 PM.	Company move to bivouac near MEAULTE.	

REPORT ON OPERATIONS

undertaken by

166th Machine Gun Company on August 9th 1916

****

1.* In accordance with verbable operations orders dictated at Brigade Headquarters at 7-0 p.m. on the 8th inst, the following orders were issued to the section officers:-

No. 1 section (Lt. Mansfield & 2nd Lt Davey) had already proceeded to the BRICQUETERIE where they remained until relieved at 4-0 p.m. on August 10th without anything of importance occurring.

No. 2 section (2nd Lt Lauder & 2nd Lt Taylor) were ordered to proceed to CASEMENT TRENCH and report to the O.C. 1/5th Kings Own: and co-operate with that battalion if necessary. As events turned out, they remained in this position until relieved at 4-0 p.m. on August 10th.

No. 3 section (Lt Slater & 2nd Lt Pratt)
The general situation and objectives were explained roughly pending the arrival of the Operation Order. The Officers in charge were ordered to attach themselves to the fourth wave in the attack but on no account to leave the present British Front line until the German line had been taken beyond doubt.
From the nature of the ground it was inadvisable to support an attack with overhead fire.
This section was ordered to report to O.C. 1/5th Loyal North Lancs: at CASEMENT TRENCH at 9-30 p.m. on the 8th inst. On arrival there the Officer in charge found that the 1/5th Loyal North Lancs: had already proceeded to the line several hours previously acting under instructions from the 164th Brigade, accordingly Lieut. Slater decided to proceed to the front line and distribute his guns over the front allotted to the 1/5th L.N.Lancs: in the attack.
Two guns under 2nd Lieut Pratt relieved two guns of the 164th Brigade at S 30 a 6.8. and S 24 c 6.3. at 12-0 midnight. The other two guns under Lieut Slater by chance alighted on and relieved two guns of the 164th Brigade on either side of the GUILLEMONT - TRONES WOOD ROAD about S 30 b 4.6. This relief was complete at 1-15 a.m. on the 9th inst.
About 4-20 a.m. the bombardment ceased for 5 mins, and Lieut. Slater observed one Company of the 1/5th South Lancs: (who had been told to make for the Quarry) advancing over the open. On arrival on the crest of the hill about 150 yards in front of the gun position in the front line this party was shot down by Machine Guns. Subsequently, as no organised wave arrived to which Lieut Slater could attach himself, he decided to improve the front line position and act on the defensive. About 5-0 a.m. word was passed down from the right that the attacking force were back in their original trenches. 2nd Lieut. Pratt (on the left) on hearing that "C" Company of the 1/5th Loyal North Lancs: was to constitute the 4th wave, attached himself to them, but as they did not attack, remained in the positions he had taken over from the 164th Brigade until relieved at 7-0 p.m. on the 10th inst.

No. 4 section (2nd Lieut Aitken & 2nd Lieut. Small)
This section was told to parade and attach itself to the 1/10th Liverpool Scottish at 8-0 p.m., and proceed with them to the line. Frontage and Objective was explained, and the same orders for attack as was given to No. 3 section.
After much delay, the section reached the sunken road at 3-0 a.m. Much difficulty was experienced at obtaining any information owing to the conglomeration of different units there.
At 4-0 a.m., finding no guns of the other Brigade to relieve, 2nd Lieut. Small took up positions behind the front line, South of ARROW HEAD COPSE in shell holes. At 4-15 a.m., he was able to move one gun into the support line at S 30 b 4.1. and another gun into the front line at S 30 d 4.9. At this time no one in the neighbourhood seemed clear as to whether the attack was to take place or not. The first wave went over at about 4-25 a.m. and soon afterwards Lt-Col. Davidson C.M.G. (1/10th Liverpool Scottish) arrived in the front line and ordered the right Machine Gun to try and engage an enemy's Machine Gun which was holding up the attack.

About 5-0 a.m., 2nd Lieut Small decided to improve the positions in the trenches and await further orders.
Two guns under 2nd Lieut Aitken got into position in shell holes behind the front line and just South of ARROW HEAD COPSE at 4-20 a.m. One Gun was immediately put out of action by a rifle bullet. Meanwhile 2nd Lieut Aitken had been wounded so Sgt Nevin who was left in charge moved the second gun to replace this. This gun had only just been mounted when the position was heavily shelled, the teams, gun, and all ammunition were put out of action. A man from the team reported that three waves of the 1/10th Liverpool Scottish went over in succession and reached the German wire which was only 100 yards East of our front line trench. There, they closed in, in order to traverse the gaps in the wire and were caught by German Machine Guns.

2. Two survivers of these two teams were then sent back by 2nd Lieut. Small. This left six guns in the line in the positions already enumerated, where they stayed until they were relieved at 8-0 p.m. on the 10th inst.

3 a. All the above Officers are of the opinion that most of the men attacking which started behind our front line, mistook our front line for the German front line.

3 b During the bombardment, German Machine Guns were very active all down our front line and particularly on the left, between the GUILLEMONT - TRONES WOOD ROAD and the Railway.

4. Total casualties in this operation were:-

Killed	5 Other Ranks
Wounded	1 Officer (2nd Lt R.R.Aitken) and 4 Other ranks, of whom two have returned to duty.
Missing	2 Other ranks.

[signature] for
Captain.
11/8/16 Commanding 166th Machine Gun Company.

CONTINUATION OF THE REPORT OF OPERATIONS OF 9TH & 10TH AUGUST 1916

On the evening of the 10th inst, the Company was relieved by the 72nd M.G.Company and moved into bivouacs E. of the PERONNE Road, no further casualties being suffered.

In accordance with orders received at 6-0 p.m. on the 12th inst. the Company moved at 7-0 p.m. in order to take over from the 165th M.G.Company -- the line South of ARROW HEAD COPSE to the left of the French.

On arrival at Battalion Headquarters I found the attack by the 165th Brigade still in progress and as the positions of the guns of the 165th M.G.Company were not definitely known, I considered it inadvisable to take over the positions that night. This arrangement was sanctioned by Brigadier General Duncan of the 165th Brigade and the Company which had reached the BRIQUETERIE Road was turned back and placed in dug-outs in the CARNOY VALLEY. It was arranged that the relief should take place at 4-0 a.m. on the 13th inst, but this was cancelled later owing to the situation in the front line still not being clear.

At 8-0 p.m. on the 13th inst, 12 guns of this Company moved up to relieve the 165th M.G.Company. Owing to the heavy shelling great difficulty was experienced in getting up to the front line and it was largely due to the action and presence of mind of No.1083 Sgt Greaves.J., that this was successfully accomplished at 11-0 p.m. with the loss of two men wounded.

The location of the guns was as follows:-

2 Guns in isolated trench of the left sector front line under 2nd Lieut Lauder.

2 Guns in support of these in MALTZ HORN FARM communication trench, under Sgt Greaves.

2 Guns in the front line right sector joining the French under 2nd Lieut Davey.

2 Guns 100 yards to the rear in support of these under Lieut. Mansfield.

2 Guns in support at Battalion Headquarters under 2nd Lieut Small.

4 Guns in CARNOY VALLEY under Lieut Slater.

2 Guns out of action on the 9th inst.

During the night of the 13th/14th inst, L/Cpl Kerr in charge of the right gun in the left sector heard and subsequently noticed a few of the enemy across the open and probably moving into shell holes quite close to the trench. Bombs were thrown at these -- the result was not observed.

The 14th inst was quiet, and the time was spent in improving the gun positions.

2nd Lieut Davey and a sniper of the 1/10th Liverpool Scottish accounted for 2 or 3 of the enemy during the day who showed themselves in the open.

The Company was relieved on the night of the 14th/15th inst by the 9th and 76th M.G.Companies of the 3rd Division No further incident of importance occurred and no further casualties were suffered.

The Company bivouaced near MANSEL COPSE.

21/8/16.

A Rowe [signature]
for
Captain.
Commanding 166th M.G.Company.

166th Machine Gun Company.

Vol 7

War Diary

for

September 1916.

—

Instructions regarding War Diaries and Intelligence Summaries are contained in F. S. Regs., Part II. and the Staff Manual respectively. Title pages will be prepared in manuscript.

WAR DIARY
or
INTELLIGENCE SUMMARY.
(Erase heading not required.)

Army Form C. 2118.

Place	Date	Hour	Summary of Events and Information	Remarks and references to Appendices
MEAULTE.	1st to 4		In bivouacs near Meaulte	
	5	2PM.	Company move to MONTAUBAN. 2 sections go in front line in DELVILLE WOOD	
	6		Casualties. 1 off. wounded 2 OR wounded and 1 other rank killed	
	7		" 1 other rank wounded.	
	8	4am	2 sections relieved 2 other sections in front line.	
	9		Operation attacked.	
	11		2 sections and transport move to bivouacs N. of BERNACOURT	
	12		In camp W. of ALBERT.	
	13		Rest of Coy. return from MONTAUBAN, relieved by 123rd Coy. No further Casualties	
	14		Training in camp.	
	15		Remained in camp – beginning of big offensive on whole front – Divn. in CORPS reserve.	
	16.		Moved into camp, little nearer ALBERT.	
	17.	1am.	Received orders to go and reconnoitre trenches at FLERS. Coy. moved to POMMIER REDOUBT near MONTAUBAN in afternoon. During the night 17/18th Coy. went into support of 165th Coy. at SWITCH, BROWN & TEA trenches	

Instructions regarding War Diaries and Intelligence Summaries are contained in F. S. Regs., Part II. and the Staff Manual respectively. Title pages will be prepared in manuscript.

WAR DIARY
or
INTELLIGENCE SUMMARY.
(*Erase heading not required.*)

Army Form C. 2118.

Place	Date	Hour	Summary of Events and Information	Remarks and references to Appendices
	18.		Took over from 165' Coy. pouring rain. 8 guns in front line. 8 in support.	
	19		Pouring rain very cold. Mud over the mens knees.	
	20.		Still rain. Conditions very bad for the men. Transport heavily shelled on the FLERS - LONGUEVAL road. Much damage done.	
	21		Much work done on our trenches, in making assembly trenches for the 165' to attack.	
	22,		Still very cold weather but no rain. GERMAN attack expected during the night but nothing came of it.	
	23		Heavily gas shelled. Coy. relieved by the 165' Coy. during the 23/24th. Move back to rest POMMIER REDOUBT.	
			Casualties during the week 1 off. wounded. 1 man missing 8 wounded none of which returned to duty.	
	24		Resting at POMMIER REDOUBT	
	25		Divn. reserve to the attack on GIRD TRENCH by the 165' Bde.	
	27.	10.45pm	Bombs dropped from enemy aeroplane on camp. Much damage done	
	28.	8 am	Move to RIBEMONT.	
	29	11.30am	Transport move to PONT. REMY. & 30' Coy entrain for PONT. REMY.	

T.134. Wt. W708-776. 500000. 4/15. Sir J. C. & S.

Report on Operations undertaken by the 166th Machine Gun Coy in co-operation with the 164th Machine Gun Coy.

1. General Plan

After consultation with the O.C. 164th Machine Gun Coy. it was arranged that from 5–7 p.m. on the 9th inst. Machine Guns should assist by keeping up continuous fire in squares T.7.a.&c. and ALE ALLEY.

2. Operations of No. 3 gun vide sketch map

At 5 p.m. the N.C.O. in charge of No. 3 gun noticed about 50 Germans lining a very shallow trench, presumably ALE ALLEY from T.13.a. 2.7. to T.13.a.6.8. They had their backs to the gun and were facing due South. Fire was opened and at least 12 were seen to drop. Subsequently until 9 p.m. small groups of men appeared. Sustained fire was not kept up owing to the fact that the N.C.O. in charge was not certain of the position of the 164 Brigade and how far their attack had progressed.

(3) Operations of No. 1 gun in No. 1 Strong Point

At about 5.50 p.m. Cpl. Roughsedge in charge of this gun noticed a few Germans moving towards ALE ALLEY from T.7.c.9.7. Fire was opened and the party dispersed. At 12.30 a.m. to-day the sentry on duty heard talking and saw figures moving about 30 yds to his front. A patrol from the 5. Lancs reported that they were Germans, so a Verey Light was sent up from a flank. From this some 15 to 20 Germans were observed, obviously having lost their way and having a consultation as to where they had to go. Fire was opened & with good result. Subsequently small parties appeared but the N.C.O. in charge of the Gun arranged that rifles should take these on, in order that his position should not be spotted. At 5 a.m. this morning No. 2395 Pte. Chew went out to discover what damage had been inflicted on the enemy during the night. 12 Germans were found together in one place, all hit by Machine Gun bullets and others were noticed in neighbouring shell holes. This same man brought in 3 prisoners on his return.

(4). Information:-

I questioned a German officer who was captured in front of No 1 Strong point and he said that his men were in shell-holes, some 50 to 60 metres from the trenches, and that he had been trying to get to ALE ALLEY but had got lost on the way.

5. Co-operation

During this operation the greatest help was given to the Machine Guns by the patrols of the 5th South Lancs.

6. Dispositions

The gun which was at S.12.d.5.7. has been moved into the new front line to a position at S.12.d.7.8.

7. General

Shelling in the centre of DELVILLE Wood, pretty heavy. One man and some gun equipment buried in INNER TRENCH. The man has been dug-out and is alright.

8. Work

Gun position No. 1 strong point have been finished and revetted with sandbags.

9. Casualties - nil

A Preme Lieut
for ~~Captain~~
Cmdg. 166 Machine Gun Coy

10.9.16.

SECRET

Vol. 8

War Diary

of

166th Machine Gun Company

for

October 1916.

Instructions regarding War Diaries and Intelligence Summaries are contained in F. S. Regs., Part II. and the Staff Manual respectively. Title pages will be prepared in manuscript.

WAR DIARY
or
~~INTELLIGENCE SUMMARY.~~
(*Erase heading not required.*)

Army Form C. 2118.

Place	Date	Hour	Summary of Events and Information	Remarks and references to Appendices
RIBEMONT.	SEPT. 30.		Move by train to LONGPRÉ and march to PONT REMY, to billets.	
	OCT 2.		MARCH to ABBEVILLE and move by train to PROVEN. Detrain & march to K camp near POPERINGHE.	
	3	4.30PM.	March to station POPERINGHE & entrain for YPRES.	
			RELIEVED 87th M.G. Coy., one section in trenches at POTIJZE, one section in trenches WIELTJE & one section at ST. JEAN.	
			One section and HDQRS. at CANAL BANK.	
	4.		Position very quiet. Enemy machine guns fairly active on ST. JEAN road every night. Enemy send a few shells into YPRES every day. Weather fair.	
			Every night fire is directed ~~on~~ from our M.G.s on the enemy dumps and roads and C.T.s	
	17		Enemy searchlights active during night. Enemy bombarded gun emplacement at WIELTJE with MINENWERFERS during 16th & 17th. PIECE OF MINNENWERFER picked up & sent in through BRIGADE for examination.	[initials]

2353 Wt. W2544/1454 700,000 5/15 D. D. & L. A.D.S.S./Forms/C. 2118.

Instructions regarding War Diaries and Intelligence Summaries are contained in F. S. Regs., Part II. and the Staff Manual respectively. Title pages will be prepared in manuscript.

WAR DIARY
or
INTELLIGENCE SUMMARY.
(Erase heading not required.)

Army Form C. 2118.

Place	Date	Hour	Summary of Events and Information	Remarks and references to Appendices
	OCT.			
YPRES.	18		Enemy bombarded trenches at WIELTJE with MINNENWERFERS. Trench badly damaged.	
	21		Enemy aeroplanes active over our lines.	
	22		2 sections relieved by 2 sections of the 164th Coy. in WIELTJE & POTIJZE. Enemy aeroplanes active during the day.	
	23		Relief completed. Company proceed to camp at BRANDHOEK. Reinforcements 6 other ranks arrived.	
	24.		Cleaning up & inspection.	
	25. to 29.		Training. Weather very wet	
	30.		Relieved 164th Coy at CANAL BANK, ST JEAN, POTIJZE & WIELTJE.	RMB
	31.		Quiet. Weather showery.	

SECRET

Vol 9

WAR DIARY

for

MONTH OF NOVEMBER 1916

of

166th MACHINE GUN COMPANY

Army Form C. 2118.

WAR DIARY
or
INTELLIGENCE SUMMARY.
(Erase heading not required.)

Instructions regarding War Diaries and Intelligence Summaries are contained in F. S. Regs., Part II. and the Staff Manual respectively. Title pages will be prepared in manuscript.

Place	Date	Hour	Summary of Events and Information	Remarks and references to Appendices
YPRES	Novr. 3	6 PM	POTIJZE WOOD shelled. Trench blown in.	
			Weather showery.	
	4"		During afternoon enemy trench mortars active.	
	9"	4 PM	Two enemy aeroplanes appeared over our lines.	
			POTIJZE WOOD slightly shelled.	
			Enemy M.G's active during each night.	
	12"		Enemy M.G's very active on front line parapets and support lines.	BGS
	13"		During the night transport was heard behind enemy lines and M.G. fire was directed on to roads. 3 Germans observed on their parapet.	
			Enemy aeroplanes active.	
			Weather very cold and wet.	
	14"		Enemy artillery active. Enemy aircraft brought down one of our observation balloons.	
			Enemy aeroplanes active during the night.	BGS

Instructions regarding War Diaries and Intelligence Summaries are contained in F. S. Regs., Part II. and the Staff Manual respectively. Title pages will be prepared in manuscript.

WAR DIARY
or
INTELLIGENCE SUMMARY.
(Erase heading not required.)

Army Form C. 2118.

Place	Date	Hour	Summary of Events and Information	Remarks and references to Appendices
YPRES	Nov. 3	6 PM	POTIJZE WOOD shelled. [illegible] blown in. Weather showery.	KS
	4		During afternoon enemy trench mortars active.	
	9	4 PM	Two enemy aeroplanes appeared over our lines. POTIJZE WOOD slightly shelled. Enemy M.G's active during each night.	
	12		Enemy M.G's very active on front line parapet, and support lines.	
	13		During the night transport was heard behind enemy lines and M.G. fire was directed on to roads. 3 Germans observed on their parapet. Enemy aeroplanes active. Weather very cold and wet.	
	14		Enemy artillery active. Enemy aircraft brought down one of our observation balloons. Enemy aeroplanes active during the night.	KKS

2353 Wt. W2544/1454 700,000 5/15 D. D. & L. A.D.S.S./Forms/C. 2118.

Army Form C. 2118.

Instructions regarding War Diaries and Intelligence Summaries are contained in F. S. Regs., Part II. and the Staff Manual respectively. Title pages will be prepared in manuscript.

WAR DIARY
or
INTELLIGENCE SUMMARY.
(Erase heading not required.)

Place	Date	Hour	Summary of Events and Information	Remarks and references to Appendices
	Nov.			
YPRES.	15		Enemy transport heard behind lines during the night. Enemy working on wire during night.	
	16		Enemy aeroplanes active during the day. ST. JEAN shelled.	
	18		Relieved by 164 M. G. Coy. Hdqrs. + 2 sections proceed to CAMP at BRANDHOEK. 1 section occupies positions in RAMPARTS, S. of MENIN GATE YPRES. 1 section occupies positions at REIGERSBURG.	[illegible]
BRANDHOEK	19 to 26.		In training. Weather cold and wet.	
	26.	4.30 p.m.	Proceed by train to YPRES. Relieve 164 M.G. Coy. on CANAL BANK, and in ST. JEAN, WIELTJE + POTIJZE.	
	26.	8.30 p.m.	Enemy sent about 15 shells which fell near gun position at C. 28.a.63.65. (Trench MAP. ST. JULIEN). Enemy transport heard during night, close behind his front line opposite WIELTJE.	
	27	6-9 p.m.	Artillery activity on both sides. Firing ceased on two	[illegible]

2353 Wt. W2544/1454 700,000 5/15 D. D. & L. A.D.S.S./Forms/C. 2118.

Instructions regarding War Diaries and Intelligence Summaries are contained in F. S. Regs., Part II. and the Staff Manual respectively. Title pages will be prepared in manuscript.

Army Form C. 2118.

WAR DIARY
or
INTELLIGENCE SUMMARY.
(Erase heading not required.)

Place	Date	Hour	Summary of Events and Information	Remarks and references to Appendices
	Nov.			
YPRES.	15		Enemy transport heard behind lines during the night. Enemy working on wire during night.	
	16		Enemy aeroplanes active during the day. ST. JEAN shelled	
	18		Relieved by 164 M. G. Coy. Hdqrs. + 2 sections proceed to CAMP at BRANDHOEK. 1 section occupies positions in RAMPARTS, S. of MENIN GATE. YPRES. 1 section occupies positions at REIGERSBURG.	BkS
ZANDHOEK	19 to 25		In training.	
		4.30pm	Proceeded by road to YPRES. Relieve 164 M.G. Coy. on CANAL BANK, and in ST. JEAN, WIELTJE + POTIJZE.	
	26	8.30pm	Enemy sent about 15 shells which fell near gun position at C. 28. a. 63. 65. (French MAP. ST. JULIEN). Enemy transport heard during night, close behind his front line opposite WIELTJE.	
	27	6-9pm	Artillery activity on both sides. Firing ceased on two	BkS

2353 Wt. W2544/1454 700,000 5/15 D. D. & L. A.D.S.S./Forms/C. 2118.

Army Form C. 2118.

Instructions regarding War Diaries and Intelligence Summaries are contained in F. S. Regs., Part II. and the Staff Manual respectively. Title pages will be prepared in manuscript.

WAR DIARY
or
INTELLIGENCE SUMMARY.
(Erase heading not required.)

Place	Date	Hour	Summary of Events and Information	Remarks and references to Appendices
			red flares being sent up.	
	28th	3.15pm	3 pigeons, flying very low, were observed to cross over from our lines to enemy lines.	
			Enemy M.G. firing during the night, was hitting our wire in front of WIELTJE.	
			Weather very cold and misty.	
	29th	~~3.45~~ 4pm 6pm	Raid was carried out by 1/10th (Scottish) King's L'pool Regt. The Machine Guns fired on to enemy trenches during the raid. Number of rounds fired 19,000.	BSS

2353 Wt. W2544/1454 700,000 5/15 D. D. & L. A.D.S.S./Forms/C. 2118.

Instructions regarding War Diaries and Intelligence Summaries are contained in F. S. Regs., Part II. and the Staff Manual respectively. Title pages will be prepared in manuscript.

WAR DIARY
or
INTELLIGENCE SUMMARY.
(Erase heading not required.)

Army Form C. 2118.

Place	Date	Hour	Summary of Events and Information	Remarks and references to Appendices
			red flares being sent up.	
	28th	3.15 pm.	3 pigeons, flying very low, were observed to cross over from our lines to enemy lines.	
			Enemy M.G. firing during the night, was hitting our wire in front of WIELTJE.	
			Weather very cold and misty.	
	29th	~~3~~4.45 p.m. to 6 p.m.	Raid was carried out by 1/10th (Scottish) King's L'pool Regt. ~~Obus~~ Maxim Guns fired on to enemy trenches during the raid. Number of rounds fired 19,000	B.B.

CONFIDENTIAL

Vol 10

War Diary

of

166th Machine Gun Coy

for period

December 1st - 31st 1916

166th MACHINE GUN COMPANY

Instructions regarding War Diaries and Intelligence Summaries are contained in F. S. Regs., Part II. and the Staff Manual respectively. Title pages will be prepared in manuscript.

WAR DIARY
~~or~~
~~INTELLIGENCE~~ SUMMARY.
(Erase heading not required.)

Army Form C. 2118.

Place	Date	Hour	Summary of Events and Information	Remarks and references to Appendices
CANAL BANK	December/16			
YPRES	1/12/16		Enemy Artillery very active.	
	2nd to 5th		Enemy Machine Guns very active during nights.	
	5th/6th		Enemy Artillery active between 10-30 a.m. & 2-45 p.m. Enemy transport heard between 4-0-5-30 p.m.	
	7th		Artillery active on both sides between 6-30 & 7-30 a.m.	
	9th		Enemy Artillery active	BRB
	12th		Enemy aeroplanes active over our lines between 8-30 & 9-0 a.m. Enemy Artillery active	
	14th		M.G. emplacements C28.3 & C28.1 were shelled. No damage done.	
	17th		Company relieved by 164 M.G.Coy. Company proceeded to camp at BRANDHOEK with the exception of one Section which went in Support at MENIN GATE YPRES	
BRANDHOEK	18th-26th		Training in Camp.	BRB
	25th		Xmas day & holiday. Artillery on both sides very quiet.	
CANAL BANK YPRES.	27th	4-10 pm	Entrained at BRANDHOEK for YPRES. Relieved the 164th M.G.Coy	
	29th		29 O.R. & one Officer from 196th M.G.Coy attached to this Coy for instruction	
	29th	1 a.m.	Two guns evacuated positions at I4b 35.40 & C28d 15.32 & took up secret positions in MILL COTS in I5a 20.70. (STJULIEN MAP 28 N.W 2)	
	30th	Noon	Enemy Artillery active. Strength 9 Officers 176 other ranks 57 animals.	BRB

T.131. Wt. W708–776. 500000. 4/15. Sir J. C. & S.

Vol XI

War Diary

of the

166 M. G. Coy.

for the period

1/1/17 to 31/1/17.

I

Instructions regarding War Diaries and Intelligence Summaries are contained in F. S. Regs., Part II. and the Staff Manual respectively. Title pages will be prepared in manuscript.

WAR DIARY
~~or~~
~~INTELLIGENCE SUMMARY.~~
(*Erase heading not required.*)

Army Form C. 2118.

Place	Date	Hour	Summary of Events and Information	Remarks and references to Appendices
CANAL BANK YPRES.	1917 JANY. 1st	5-30 pm.	Our Artillery & trench mortars bombarded the enemy's trenches two of our Machine Guns co-operating, firing all the night to hinder enemy from rebuilding damaged trenches.	
"	2nd		During the greater part of the morning the enemy shelled the "Dead End" (Canal bank) & M.G. Coy area.	
"	3. "	3-0 pm.	Enemy shell hit a Company dugout on Canal bank, blowing the front of the dug-out in, killing one O.R. & wounding three O.Rs.	
"	5th	3-0 to 4-0 pm	Enemy Artillery very active during this period, about twelve shells dropped around Company H.Qs, wounding two O.Rs.	
"	7th	3.0 a.m.	Concentrated enemy fire on our front line trenches N. of WIELTJE Intermittent shelling of Ypres.	
"	10th	3-0 to 6-0 pm.	Company H.Qs subjected to fire from enemy's heavy artillery. Nine (9) of our Machine Guns took part in raid by 1/5th L. N. Lancs Rt. One of our emplacements was blown in & one gun put out of action.	[signature]

(continued)

T.134. Wt. W708-776. 500000. 4/15. Sir J. C. & S.

II (continued)

Instructions regarding War Diaries and Intelligence Summaries are contained in F. S. Regs., Part II. and the Staff Manual respectively. Title pages will be prepared in manuscript.

WAR DIARY

~~or~~

~~INTELLIGENCE SUMMARY.~~

(Erase heading not required.)

Army Form C. 2118.

Place	Date	Hour	Summary of Events and Information	Remarks and references to Appendices
CANAL BANK YPRES.	1917 JANY. 12th	p.m. 8.45 to 9.15 p.m.	Enemy bombarded our right battalion front, in POTIJZE Sector. In reply to the "S.O.S." our artillery opened fire, & Machine Guns immediately opened out on German communication trenches of that Sector. No raid was made.	
	14th		Company relieved by 118th M.G. Coy & proceeded to "L" Camp, & stayed there one day.	
	16th	am 10.30	Company entrained at St. JAHNSTON BIEZEN ~~at 10.30~~ & proceeded to BOLLEZEELE.	
BOLLEZEELE	17th to 31st		Started the Training Scheme, which was still in progress at the end of the month (31st Jany. 1917)	

A Rowe Lt
for Commanding 166 Machine Gun Coy.

31.1.17.

CONFIDENTIAL

Vol 12.

War Diary

of

166th M. G. Coy

for the period

1st to 28th February 1917

Instructions regarding War Diaries and Intelligence Summaries are contained in F. S. Regs., Part II. and the Staff Manual respectively. Title pages will be prepared in manuscript.

WAR DIARY
or
~~INTELLIGENCE SUMMARY.~~

(Erase heading not required.)

Army Form C. 2118.

Place	Date	Hour	Summary of Events and Information	Remarks and references to Appendices
BOLLEZEELE	1st to 4th Feby		This Company completed its Period of Training in Advanced Drill and Open Warfare, together with Training of Signallers and Runners. During the period of Training the Company was inspected by the Brigadier General on 2 or 3 Occasions.	R.B.
	4th Feby.	9am.	The Company entrained at BOLLEZEELE and proceeded to CHEESE MARKET STATION. POPERINGHE where Company detrained and marched to "S" Camp. ELVERDINGHE	
	4th to 17th Feby.		During the time stationed at "S" Camp, Company was in Division Reserve, training in Open War-fare carried on	
	12th		a field day during which the G.O.C. 55th Division inspected the Company.	R.B.
	17th.		Marched from "S" Camp to BRANDHOEK STATION where Company entrained for YPRES, after detraining marched into the line (WIELTJE SECTOR). Headquarters taking up BILLETS in the CANAL BANK. YPRES. 12 guns being in the line.	

T.134. Wt. W708–776. 500000. 4/15. Sir J. C. & S.

Instructions regarding War Diaries and Intelligence Summaries are contained in F. S. Regs., Part II. and the Staff Manual respectively. Title pages will be prepared in manuscript.

WAR DIARY
or
~~INTELLIGENCE SUMMARY.~~
(Erase heading not required.)

Army Form C. 2118.

Place	Date	Hour	Summary of Events and Information	Remarks and references to Appendices
CANAL BANK YPRES.	18th to 25 Feby		No Casualties to the Company during period in the line. Enemy abnormally quiet. Very foggy weather.	BB
	25 Feby		Company was relieved in WIELTJE SECTOR by the 16th MACHINE GUN COMPANY., after which 2 Sections marched to YPRES. STATION, remaining 2 Sections took up RESERVE POSITIONS. in the RAMPARTS, and KAAIE SALIENT. YPRES. 2 Sections entrained for BRANDHOEK where ~~Company~~ they detrained & proceeded to Huts at BRANDHOEK.	
	26th Feby		Cleaning up.	BB
	27-28		Training.	

[signature] Capt.
O.C 166th Machine Gun Coy

T.2134. Wt. W768-776. 500000. 4/15. Sir J. C. & S.

Vol 13

War Diary

of the

166th M. G. Coy

for the period

1st to 31st March

1917.

Instructions regarding War Diaries and Intelligence Summaries are contained in F. S. Regs., Part II. and the Staff Manual respectively. Title pages will be prepared in manuscript.

WAR DIARY
or
INTELLIGENCE SUMMARY.
(Erase heading not required.)

Army Form C. 2118.

Place	Date	Hour	Summary of Events and Information	Remarks and references to Appendices
BRANHOEK.	Ma.			
28 Feb 16 – 6th Mar.			2. Sections of Company doing training at Camp at BRANDHOEK, in Advanced Drill, Revolver practise and Gas Drill.	
	March 6/7.		The 2 Sections in RESERVE at RAMPARTS, YPRES and 2 Sections at Camp. BRANDHOEK marched with Limbers to RAILWOOD SECTOR, Head quarters taking up Billets in SCHOOL HOUSE ECOLE. Here the Company had 16 guns in the line during a period of 10 days. In this time the Company only had one casualty. Enemy sprung 2 mines in RAILWAY WOOD.	
	17		On this night the Company proceeded across country to take up positions with 16 guns in the WIELTJE Sector. Headquarters being on the CANAL BANK, YPRES.	
	24.		After 10 days in this sector the Company	

Instructions regarding War Diaries and Intelligence Summaries are contained in F. S. Regs., Part II. and the Staff Manual respectively. Title pages will be prepared in manuscript.

WAR DIARY
or
INTELLIGENCE SUMMARY.
(Erase heading not required.)

Army Form C. 2118.

Place	Date	Hour	Summary of Events and Information	Remarks and references to Appendices
	March			
			was relieved by the 16th Machine Gun Company 2 Sections moving down to "L" Lines ELVERDINGHE in Reserve, the other two sections returning to Camp at BRANDHOEK.	
BRANDHOEK	28		Training of these two Sections in the following took place viz. Advanced Drill, practising taking up positions and moving across country with Pack Animals, Revolver Drill, Gas Drill and Firing on 30 yards Range.	
			R. M. Buckley Captain 166th Machine Gun Coy.	
31/3/17				

CONFIDENTIAL

Vol 14

War Diary

of

166th Machine Gun Coy

for the period

April 1st to 30th 1917

WAR DIARY
or
~~INTELLIGENCE SUMMARY.~~
(Erase heading not required.)

Army Form C. 2118.

Instructions regarding War Diaries and Intelligence Summaries are contained in F. S. Regs., Part II. and the Staff Manual respectively. Title pages will be prepared in manuscript.

Place	Date	Hour	Summary of Events and Information	Remarks and references to Appendices
BRANDHOEK [illegible]	1st to 6th april.		Training in advanced Machine Gun Work continued with.	
	6/7		Company marched through YPRES to the line. RIGHT BRIGADE SECTOR (16 Guns in the line occupying RAILWAY WOOD and POTIJZE WOOD SECTORS. Headquarters taking up Billets in the School House ECOLE. During the period in this SECTOR (being 10 days) our Machine Guns were fairly active in cooperation with Artillery in bombarding the Enemy's trenches	
YPRES.	16/7		In the evening the Company was relieved in the RIGHT BRIGADE SECTOR by the 165th M. G. Coy. and moved across country to occupy M.G. Positions in the LEFT BRIGADE SECTOR here relieving the 164th M.G. Coy. (13 Guns being in the line and 3 Guns with Headquarters in DUG-OUTS on CANAL BANK, YPRES.	
	18		From this date onward Hostile aircraft being very active and were on many occasions targets for our Machine	

2353 Wt. W2544/1454 700,000 5/15 D. D. & L. A.D.S.S./Forms/C. 2118.

Instructions regarding War Diaries and Intelligence Summaries are contained in F. S. Regs., Part II. and the Staff Manual respectively. Title pages will be prepared in manuscript.

WAR DIARY
or
INTELLIGENCE SUMMARY.
(Erase heading not required.)

Army Form C. 2118.

Place	Date	Hour	Summary of Events and Information	Remarks and references to Appendices
YPRES.	April 18		Guns. Visibility being for the most part good enabled small parties of the Enemy to be observed and which were dispersed by our Machine Gun Fire	
	23rd		Four Guns of the 196th M.G. Coy attached to us and 3 more positions taken over making 16 Guns in the line	
	27th		Both Hostile and own Aircraft very Active. Visibility Good	
	29th/30	12.30 am	An Enterprise took place by the Brigade on our Left and Enemys retaliation was very week.	

30/4/17

[signature]
Captain
Commanding, 166th M. G. Coy

2353 Wt. W2544/1454 700,000 5/15 D. D. & L. A.D.S.S./Forms/C. 2118.

CONFIDENTIAL.

Vol 15

War Diary

of

166 M. G. Coy

for the period

May 1st - 31st, 1917

Instructions regarding War Diaries and Intelligence Summaries are contained in F. S. Regs., Part II. and the Staff Manual respectively. Title pages will be prepared in manuscript.

Army Form C. 2118.

WAR DIARY
or
~~INTELLIGENCE SUMMARY.~~
(Erase heading not required.)

Place	Date	Hour	Summary of Events and Information	Remarks and references to Appendices
	May			
YPRES.	1/3rd		Brigadier General F. G. Lewis C.B. C.M.G. assumed Command of the 166th Infantry Brigade on 25th April 1917 vice Brigadier General L.F. Green-Wilkinson (to England)	
			Company still holding positions in the LEFT BRIGADE SECTOR Enemy shelled heavily the PRISON YPRES. and vicinity, causing some Casualties	
	4		During the day KAAIE SALIENT was intermittently shelled by the Enemy with 8" and 5'9 shells.	
	6/7		In the evening the Company was relieved in the LEFT BRIGADE SECTOR by the 164th Machine Gun Company and proceeded to H Camp near BRANDHOEK.	
	9		Company marched from this Camp to ST. JAN. TER BIEZEN in the afternoon and was billeted in Barns and Tents outside this village.	
	10/12		Company doing training in Advanced Drill and M.G. Barrage Drill etc.	[illegible]

2353 Wt. W2544/1454 700,000 5/15 D. D. & L. A.D.S.S./Forms/C. 2118.

Instructions regarding War Diaries and Intelligence Summaries are contained in F. S. Regs., Part II. and the Staff Manual respectively. Title pages will be prepared in manuscript.

WAR DIARY
or
~~INTELLIGENCE SUMMARY~~.
(Erase heading not required.)

Army Form C. 2118.

Place	Date	Hour	Summary of Events and Information	Remarks and references to Appendices
ST-JAN-TER-BIEZEN	May 13	10.0 am	(Sunday) Company attended the Brigade Church Parade of ST-JAN-TER-BIEZEN	
	14	2.30 pm	The Brigadier General Commanding inspected the Company together with Sections Limbers.	
	15		Further Company Training was carried out	
	16		During the Day Company prepared to proceed to POPERINGHE where Company entrained for YPRES. On arrival at YPRES, detrained and marched to positions in the RIGHT BRIGADE SECTOR there, relieving the 165th M.G. Coy. Headquarters at the ECOLE (School House) 15 guns being in the line and 4 guns of the 196th M.G. Coy attached to this Company in the positions in the RAMPARTS, YPRES. One Gun of this Company at the Headquarters. ECOLE.	
	19.		Captain J.A. Gillies assumed Command of this Company vice Captain R.M. Buckley to Machine Gun Corps Base Depot, CAMIERS.	

2353 Wt. W2544/1454 700,000 5/15 D. D. & L. A.D.S.S./Forms/C. 2118.

Instructions regarding War Diaries and Intelligence Summaries are contained in F. S. Regs., Part II. and the Staff Manual respectively. Title pages will be prepared in manuscript.

WAR DIARY
or
~~INTELLIGENCE SUMMARY.~~

(Erase heading not required.)

Army Form C. 2118.

Place	Date	Hour	Summary of Events and Information	Remarks and references to Appendices
YPRES.	20.		During the Day Enemy shelled intermittently the vicinity of the ECOLE with heavies.	
			Our Anti-aircraft guns very active on Hostile aircraft.	
	20/26		During this period Enemy shelled YPRES. particularly in the vicinity of the PRISON	
	27		The RAMPARTS and MENIN GATE were very heavily shelled by the Enemy with heavies	
	28		Enemy shelled very heavily the vicinity of the ASYLUM setting a large building ablaze. Enemy also paid much ~~attenti~~ attention to the transport causing heavy casualties in Horses & men. Hostile Aeroplane brought down by one of our guns. (machine) Our Artillery retaliated and succeeded in blowing up a large Enemy Dump. ~~He blew~~ a large mine, & no action by enemy	
	31		Inter Section relief with the 196th M.G. Coy and this Company.	

A Rome Lieut
For O.C. 166 M.G. Coy

2353 Wt. W2544/1454 700,000 5/15 D. D. & L. A.D.S.S./Forms/C. 2118.

CONFIDENTIAL

Vol 16

War Diary

of

166th M. G. Coy

for the period

June 1st to June 30th, 1917

Instructions regarding War Diaries and Intelligence Summaries are contained in F. S. Regs., Part II. and the Staff Manual respectively. Title pages will be prepared in manuscript.

WAR DIARY
or
~~INTELLIGENCE SUMMARY.~~
(Erase heading not required.)

Army Form C. 2118.

166th Machine Gun Coy

Place	Date	Hour	Summary of Events and Information	Remarks and references to Appendices
June Ypres.	1917 1st		Company still holding positions in RIGHT BRIGADE SECTOR Headquarters being in the Headmasters House ECOLE. During this period Enemy bombarded the vicinity of the ECOLE, MENIN ROAD and GATE. also YPRES with Gas shells and Lachrymatory shells intermittently throughout the night	
	6/10		Enemy Active on RAMPARTS. YPRES. causing some casualties to animals of transport. Two or three small mines were blown by us and during the earlier hours of the morning Enemy blew up 4 or 5 small mines. Considerable activity on our trenches by the Enemy and one direct hit was obtained upon a MG Dugout (Hell Fire Corner) causing 2 casualties.	
	14		Eight MG positions occupied by this Company were relieved in the RAILWAY WOOD SECTOR by the 24th MG Coy	

2353 Wt. W2544/1454 700,000 5/15 D. D. & L. A.D.S.S./Forms/C. 2118.

Instructions regarding War Diaries and Intelligence Summaries are contained in F. S. Regs., Part II. and the Staff Manual respectively. Title pages will be prepared in manuscript.

WAR DIARY
or
INTELLIGENCE SUMMARY.
(Erase heading not required.)

Army Form C. 2118.

16th Machine Gun Coy

Place	Date	Hour	Summary of Events and Information	Remarks and references to Appendices
	June 1917			
POTIJZE	14th		Headquarters then moved to POTIJZE ROAD DUG-OUTS and 5 M.G. POSITIONS were taken over by Teams of this Company in the POTIJZE SECTOR from the 65 M.G. Company. A great increase of Aerial activity during the remainder of the time in the line - 12 guns being in the line	
	19.		Company was relieved in this Sector by the 46th M.G. Coy. The Company then proceeded by Sections to OVERY CAMP off the VLAMERTINGHE - YPRES. ROAD. Here under Canvas for 2 days. In these two days Enemy shelled the adjoining 50 Camps with high velocity Shells, quite a number of them proving "BLINDS".	
	22		Company then marched from OVERY CAMP to the STATION POPERINGHE and entrained at 11 A.M. am for ST OMER. Here detraining and proceeding by Route march to QUELMES. in BILLETS.	

T.131. Wt. W708-776. 500000. 4/15. Sir J. C. & S.

Instructions regarding War Diaries and Intelligence Summaries are contained in F. S. Regs., Part II. and the Staff Manual respectively. Title pages will be prepared in manuscript.

WAR DIARY
or
INTELLIGENCE SUMMARY.
(Erase heading not required.)

Army Form C. 2118.

166th Machine Gun Coy

Place	Date	Hour	Summary of Events and Information	Remarks and references to Appendices
June 1917				
QUELMES	23/30		Company commenced a period of training	
			A Rowe Major 166 M.G. Coy	

Vol 17

War Diary

of the

166th M. G. Coy:

for the period

1st July to 31st July

1917.

Instructions regarding War Diaries and Intelligence Summaries are contained in F. S. Regs., Part II. and the Staff Manual respectively. Title pages will be prepared in manuscript.

WAR DIARY
or
~~INTELLIGENCE~~ SUMMARY.
(Erase heading not required.)

Army Form C. 2118.

166th Machine Gun Company
B.E.F.

Place	Date	Hour	Summary of Events and Information	Remarks and references to Appendices
QUELMES	1st/6th		Company carrying out programme of training for Offensive Action. Hours of training, being 4 hours per day the remainder of the day being devoted to Games &c.	
	6		Company exercised with Units in the Brigade for the Attack.	
	7.		Tanks and Aeroplanes, co-operating with Brigade Schemes Brigade Sports held on the Football Field (Sunday) at QUELMES. This Company gaining prizes in several Events.	
	19		Preparing to move (the packing of Limbers &c Transport moving by 9.0. A.m.)	
	20.		Company less transport marched off at 6.15. am by Route March to ST. OMER there entraining for HOPOUTRE. Here the Company detrained and 2. Sections proceeded to BEDOUIN CAMP and the remaining 2. Sections together with H.Qrs to RED ROSE CAMP. off the VLAMERTINGHE – YPRES Road.	

T.134. Wt. W708–776. 500000. 4/15. Sir J. C. & S.

Instructions regarding War Diaries and Intelligence Summaries are contained in F. S. Regs., Part II. and the Staff Manual respectively. Title pages will be prepared in manuscript.

WAR DIARY
or
~~INTELLIGENCE~~ SUMMARY.
(*Erase heading not required.*)

Army Form C. 2118.

166th Machine Gun Coy.

B.E.F.

Place	Date	Hour	Summary of Events and Information	Remarks and references to Appendices
	July			
YPRES	20.		The personnel of Head Qrs and 2 Sections rested at RED ROSE CAMP for a few hours, prior to going to the Line. HEAD QRS. taking up Billet on the CANAL BANK. YPRES.	
			10 Guns being in the line in M.G. Positions	
	21/22		Harassing Fire on the Enemy's Trenches carried out by 4 Guns. night and Day. Approximate number of Rounds fired per day being 28.000.	
			Enemy continued to Bombard the CANAL BANK and Back AREAS with Heavies, also Phosgene and Mustard Oil Gas Shells, inflicting many casualties in the Line several of this Company, including 2 Officers.	
			During the period up to the present in the line, Enemy, Aeroplanes were very active and flying very low over our trenches.	
			In some cases BOMBS. were dropped in our own lines from Hostile Aircraft.	

T.131. Wt. W708-776. 500000. 4/15. Sir J. C. & S.

Instructions regarding War Diaries and Intelligence Summaries are contained in F. S. Regs., Part II. and the Staff Manual respectively. Title pages will be prepared in manuscript.

WAR DIARY
or
INTELLIGENCE SUMMARY.
(Erase heading not required.)

Army Form C. 2118.

166th Machine Gun Coy. B.E.F.

Place	Date	Hour	Summary of Events and Information	Remarks and references to Appendices
	July.			
YPRES.	22/23.		Batteries in the KAAIE SALIENT and Back AREAS were heavily shelled by the Enemy. Gas Shells also being fired.	
	24		Enemy very active on our Trenches, again causing some casualties, One of our Machine Guns being put out of action killing ~~2~~ 1 man of the Gun Team and wounding 2 ~~two dead~~. (M.G. position in LIVERPOOL TRENCH)	
		about 12.30 pm	The Enemy set ~~[illegible]~~ on fire a small DUMP on the CANAL BANK. (DEAD END).	
	25.		Enemy less active with Gas Shells.	
			Our Machine Guns fired in conjunction with Daylight Raid carried out on DIVISIONAL FRONT at 1 pm. From 1.35 pm LONE TR. CONGREVE WALK, PROWSE, OXFORD and Front Line Trenches were heavily shelled. Several of our Batteries were deliberately shelled during the day, damage being caused to some of our guns. The DEAD END LOCK GATES and Canal Bank were shelled.	

Instructions regarding War Diaries and Intelligence Summaries are contained in F. S. Regs., Part II. and the Staff Manual respectively. Title pages will be prepared in manuscript.

WAR DIARY
or
INTELLIGENCE SUMMARY.
(Erase heading not required.)

Army Form C. 2118.

166th Machine Gun Coy
B.E.F.

Place	Date	Hour	Summary of Events and Information	Remarks and references to Appendices
	July			
YPRES.	26		During the day Enemy much quieter than on previous days. Both Hostile and our own aircraft were very active.	
	26/27	9pm	Enemy again very active on DEAD END. LOCK GATES of CANAL BANK. Some shells fell in close proximity to the Company BILLETS on the CANAL BANK but causing little or no damage. During the period so far spent in the line Enemy Machine Guns were abnormally quiet.	
	28		Our Machine Guns continuing a programme of Harassing Fire night and Day upon the Enemies Trenches. The Artillery firing on his Back Area.	
	29	8.30pm	Headquarters on CANAL BANK moved up to LA BRIQUE. Enemy continuing to shell CANAL BANK. LA BRIQUE and the usual BACK AREAS.	
	30.		Headquarters leaving LA BRIQUE for WIELTJE this being,	

Instructions regarding War Diaries and Intelligence Summaries are contained in F. S. Regs., Part II. and the Staff Manual respectively. Title pages will be prepared in manuscript.

WAR DIARY
or
INTELLIGENCE SUMMARY.
(Erase heading not required.)

Army Form C. 2118.

Place	Date	Hour	Summary of Events and Information	Remarks and references to Appendices
WIELTJE.			Company Headquarters for the ATTACK.	
	31.	3.50am	At this hour the ATTACK was launched. 2. M. Guns being attached to each BATTALION and 8. Machine Guns doing BARRAGE FIRE	

[signature] Capt.
O.C. 166 M.G. Coy

T.2134. Wt. W708-776. 500000. 4/15. Sir J. C. & S.

Vol 18

War Diary

of

166th M.G. Co

for period

1st to 31st August, 1917.

Instructions regarding War Diaries and Intelligence Summaries are contained in F. S. Regs., Part II. and the Staff Manual respectively. Title pages will be prepared in manuscript.

WAR DIARY
or
~~INTELLIGENCE SUMMARY.~~
(Erase heading not required.)

Army Form C. 2118.

166th Machine Gun Coy

Place	Date	Hour	Summary of Events and Information	Remarks and references to Appendices
	August			
WIELTJE.	1st		After all Objectives had been gained by the Division our troops were obliged owing to the Enemy pressing hard, and other circumstances, to fall back on to the BLACK LINE, which was by this time consolidated.	
			The Casualties to this Company were heavy being chiefly inflicted upon the personnel of the Barrage Machine Guns, which had established itself upon the Banks of the STEENBEKE. 8 Guns of this Company and 8 Guns of the 196th M.G. Coy, the latter being attached to this Company formed "S" Battery.	
			The Enemy placed his Barrage of Heavies on this spot viz the STEENBEKE.	
			Good work was executed by the above Battery. One Team firing 15 Belts at a very close range and were observed to cause numbers of casualties to the Enemy's forces advancing.	
			The Battery's Transport also rendered valuable aid ~~to the~~ by the timely assistance in the conveying of S.A.A. forward under Heavy Barrage Fire of the Enemy.	
			During the second journey the Transport Officer (Lieut. T. Dixon) was badly wounded.	

A7092. Wt. W128.9/M1293. 750,000. 1/17. D. D & L., Ltd. Forms/C2118/14.

Instructions regarding War Diaries and Intelligence Summaries are contained in F. S. Regs., Part II. and the Staff Manual respectively. Title pages will be prepared in manuscript.

WAR DIARY
or
INTELLIGENCE SUMMARY.
(*Erase heading not required.*)

Army Form C. 2118.

166 Machine Gun Company

Place	Date	Hour	Summary of Events and Information	Remarks and references to Appendices
			All the Pack Animals were killed and the T.O's Charger wounded. Several casualties were sustained by the Transport personnel, which occurred during the journey forward to the STEENBEEK.	
			The progress of operations after the first forward move was hampered considerably owing to the inclement weather making the traversing of the ground very difficult.	
	2/3		The Brigades in this Division were relieved in the line by Brigades of the 36th Division. This Company retaining M.G. positions in the line until the following evening when we were relieved by teams of the 107th M.G. Coy and 109th M.G. Coy.	A Power [illegible]
			In addition to the Company's full compliment of Guns being relieved 3 Vickers Guns and 2 German Guns were also brought out of the line.	
			Limbers conveyed the personnel from	

A7092. Wt. W12839/M1293. 750,000. 1/17. D. D & L., Ltd. Forms/C2118/14.

Instructions regarding War Diaries and Intelligence Summaries are contained in F. S. Regs., Part II. and the Staff Manual respectively. Title pages will be prepared in manuscript.

WAR DIARY
or
INTELLIGENCE SUMMARY.
(Erase heading not required.)

Army Form C. 2118.

166 Machine Gun Coy

Place	Date	Hour	Summary of Events and Information	Remarks and references to Appendices
			ST JEAN to [illegible] at [illegible]. [illegible] had [illegible] [illegible] to K Camp.	
	4		The whole day was spent in cleaning up generally.	
	5		Company [illegible] moved by [illegible] from [illegible] ABEELE and detrained at AUDRICQ [illegible] conveyed by [illegible] to [illegible] [illegible] of accommodation at [illegible] [illegible]	
	7	10.30	marched to NORDAUSQUE. At this village during the period of rest company were employed in Section training and Physical training. Transport animals and vehicles were inspected together with other units in the Brigade by the B.G.C. ~~Commanding~~	
	19		(Sunday) Brigade Church parade	
			During this period at NORDAUSQUE much time being allotted to Cross Country Running & Sport	A. Ross [illegible]

A7092. Wt. W128,9/M1293. 750,000. 1/17. D. D & L., Ltd. Forms/C2118/14.

Instructions regarding War Diaries and Intelligence Summaries are contained in F. S. Regs., Part II. and the Staff Manual respectively. Title pages will be prepared in manuscript.

WAR DIARY
or
INTELLIGENCE SUMMARY.
(Erase heading not required.)

Army Form C. 2118.

16 Machine Gun Coy (?)

Place	Date	Hour	Summary of Events and Information	Remarks and references to Appendices
NORDAUSQUES (?)			etc arranged with [illegible] units. Officers and N.C.O.s being granted 1 days leave to CALAIS proceeding by the 10.20 am train from NORDAUSQUES [illegible] and [illegible] the same day. [illegible] Company [illegible] sections [illegible] [illegible] Each evening [illegible] [illegible] [illegible] for [illegible] held [illegible] [illegible] [illegible] section [illegible] [illegible] The following Officers were awarded the MILITARY CROSS for [illegible] together with 3 other Ranks who were awarded the Military Medal. Award of these honours was made in Company Orders for 25/1/18 (?)	[illegible signature]
	21/25			

A;092 Wt. W128;9/M1293. 750,000. 1/17. D. D & L., Ltd. Forms/C2118/14.

Instructions regarding War Diaries and Intelligence Summaries are contained in F. S. Regs., Part II. and the Staff Manual respectively. Title pages will be prepared in manuscript.

WAR DIARY
or
~~INTELLIGENCE~~ SUMMARY.
(Erase heading not required.)

Army Form C. 2118.

166th Machine Gun Company

Place	Date	Hour	Summary of Events and Information	Remarks and references to Appendices
	August			
NORDAUSQUES	26th		the Distribution of these awards being postponed until Sunday 2nd Sept.	
	27/31		During this period Brigade Schemes were programmed but were not carried [illegible] owing to the inclement weather.	
			A Rowe Lieut Comndg 166 M.G. Coy.	A Rowe Lieut

A.5092 Wt. W1289/M1293 750,000. 1/17. D. D & L., Ltd. Forms/C2118/14.

166/5·5

CONFIDENTIAL

Vol 19

WAR DIARY

OF

166TH M.G. COY

FOR PERIOD

1/9/17 — 30/9/17

September 1917

WAR DIARY
or
~~INTELLIGENCE SUMMARY.~~
(Erase heading not required.)

Army Form C. 2118.

66th Machine Gun Coy

Instructions regarding War Diaries and Intelligence Summaries are contained in F. S. Regs., Part II. and the Staff Manual respectively. Title pages will be prepared in manuscript.

Place	Date	Hour	Summary of Events and Information	Remarks and references to Appendices
			Lieut A. Rowe assumes Command of Company during the absence of Capt. [illegible]	[illegible] to M.G. School CAMIERS
NORDAUSQUES	2nd		(Sunday). The G.O.C. presented ribands to Officers and Men awarded Decorations for Gallantry and Devotion to Duty during ~~recent~~ operations on 31st July. Brigade Rifle meeting took place after the above event.	
	6.		Divisional Horse Show was held in which the Coy exhibited 1 Limber and Team, and gaining 2nd prize for Smartness of Turnout &c. The Show was quite a success but unfortunately was obliged to close earlier than was programmed owing to the weather conditions hampering the progress of same.	
	7		Practising of Barrage Machine Gun work.	
	9.		Brigade Church parade. After the Service was over the B.G.C. presented ribands to Officers and Men awarded Decorations for Gallantry &c during operations on above date who did not receive them on the 2nd inst. Prizes for Rifle meeting held last Sunday were presented by the B.G.C. also.	A Rowe Lt

Instructions regarding War Diaries and Intelligence Summaries are contained in F. S. Regs., Part II. and the Staff Manual respectively. Title pages will be prepared in manuscript.

WAR DIARY
or
~~INTELLIGENCE SUMMARY.~~
(Erase heading not required.)

166th Machine Gun Coy

Army Form C. 2118.

Place	Date	Hour	Summary of Events and Information	Remarks and references to Appendices
NORDAUSQUE	10		Company's programme for the Day included Physical training under C.S.M. BINKS (166 Infy Bde P.T. & B.F. Instructor) and field firing on GOEMY RANGE.	
	14		Company marched from NORDAUSQUES to AUDRICQ, here entraining for PESELHOEK. Arrived at this Siding about 10 p.m. and proceeded on foot to GOLDFISH CHATEAU, YPRES NORTH AREA. Here the Company rested over night and the following day proceeded to	
	15		positions in the line at 6 p.m. – The front on which the attack was to take place. Company Head qrs being situate at No 25 Dug out WIELTJE.	
	18		On this night the Company was withdrawn from the line to ST JEAN area and spent the rest of the night and the following day in ST JEAN VILLAGE.	
	19.		Section Officers reconnoitred the proposed Barrage positions and marked out the sites to be occupied	

Instructions regarding War Diaries and Intelligence Summaries are contained in F. S. Regs., Part II. and the Staff Manual respectively. Title pages will be prepared in manuscript.

WAR DIARY
or
INTELLIGENCE SUMMARY.
(Erase heading not required.)

Army Form C. 2118.

Place	Date	Hour	Summary of Events and Information	Remarks and references to Appendices
ST JEAN			by each gun	
	19/20.	11pm	Teams equipped with Guns, Tripods, Belt Boxes etc on Limbers, left ST JEAN for the line. All Guns were placed in position, aiming posts erected and were dug in by 2.0 am. 20th inst. Shortly before Zero one Team sustained 6. Casualties i.e. 4 killed and 2 wounded. The Gun lowerer being undamaged. Zero hour for the attack being 5.40 am.	
	20.		The Company Artificer with a supply of Spare Barrels established a Repair Workshop at ST JEAN where there were also 2 Cyclists to act as messengers for the Transport Lines	[illegible]
			At. 5.40 am after a 24 hours bombardment the attack was launched on the Enemy's lines in conjunction with the Corps on our ~~Right~~ Left and the Army on our ~~Left~~ Right.	
			Machine Gun Barrage carried out according to Programme, approximate number of rounds fired	

D. D. & L., London, E.C. (A8004) Wt W1771/M2031 750,000 5/17 Sch. 52 Forms/C2118/14

Instructions regarding War Diaries and Intelligence Summaries are contained in F. S. Regs., Part II. and the Staff Manual respectively. Title pages will be prepared in manuscript.

WAR DIARY
or
INTELLIGENCE SUMMARY.
(Erase heading not required.)

Army Form C. 2118.

Place	Date	Hour	Summary of Events and Information	Remarks and references to Appendices
			being 100,000 Rounds.	
			3 Guns were put out of action which were replaced by 2 from ST JEAN.	
			Our attack met with considerable success along the whole front.	
	20/22		During this time the Enemy made several local Counter attacks but these were fortunately broken up by our Artillery and Machine Gun fire	
		4 pm	At this hour the Machine Guns co-operated with Artillery in a practice Barrage firing 16000 rounds and they also cooperated with the Artillery at 6 pm on the same day, 32,000 rounds being fired.	
		8.57 pm	During a quiet spell the S.O.S. Rocket was observed on the left of our front. All guns opened fire	
			On the night of the 23rd the Company were relieved on	

D. D. & L., London, E.C. (A8004) Wt W1771/M2031 750,000 5/17 Sch. 52 Forms/C2118/14

September 1917

WAR DIARY
or
INTELLIGENCE SUMMARY.
(Erase heading not required.)

Army Form C. 2118.

Instructions regarding War Diaries and Intelligence Summaries are contained in F. S. Regs., Part II. and the Staff Manual respectively. Title pages will be prepared in manuscript.

166. Machine Gun Coy

Place	Date	Hour	Summary of Events and Information	Remarks and references to Appendices
YPRES.			the front and proceeded to ST. JEAN whence they were conveyed in Limbers to GOLDFISH CHATEAU, YPRES, NORTH AREA.	
			After Breakfast Company packed. Limbers &c and prepared to move.	
			Company moved off and proceeded to POPERINGHE to Billets in Tents at WATOU. Area. No. 2. At this Camp. Company remained until the 25th inst.	
	25		Transport departed at 2.30pm for PROVEN. STATION The remainder of the Company proceeding about 6pm by Route March, via POPERINGHE - PROVEN ROAD and entrained at PROVEN STA at 8 K. pm on 25 inst.	
			Company journeyed by Train through the night and arriving at MIRAMONT at about 8.30 Am on the 26th inst.	
	26.	9.30	Breakfast was prepared after which the Company together with Transport proceed to BEAULENCOURT by Route March, passing through the villages of	

D. D. & L., London, E.C. (A5004) Wt W1771/M2091 750,000 5/17 Sch. 52 Forms/C2118/14

September 1917

Instructions regarding War Diaries and Intelligence Summaries are contained in F. S. Regs., Part II. and the Staff Manual respectively. Title pages will be prepared in manuscript.

WAR DIARY
or
~~INTELLIGENCE SUMMARY.~~
(Erase heading not required.)

16th Machine Gun Coy

Army Form C. 2118.

Place	Date	Hour	Summary of Events and Information	Remarks and references to Appendices
			ACHIET-LE PETIT, ACHIET LE GRAND, BIERVILLERS and arriving at BEAULENCOURT at about 2.30 pm.	
	24		Whilst at the above place the company had several Route Marches of short periods. Here the company was billeted in Huts.	
	28		Company moved from BEAULENCOURT to AIZECOURT-LE BAS by Route March resting here over night. The Transport proceeded to a bombing ground nearer to EPEHY. The company moving from AIZECOURT-LE-BAS and resting on Route to have TEA after the	
	30.		Tea. the journey to the line was resumed. Coy Hd. Qrs being in PARRS BANK (PIGEON RAVINE)	
			During the night things generally were very quiet ~~during the night~~ and following day.	[illegible]

D. D. & L., London, E.C.
(A8004) Wt W1771/M2031 750,000 5/17 Sch. 52 Forms/C2118/14

Vol 20

War Diary
of the
166th M. G. Coy.
for the period
1st to 31st October, 1917.

Instructions regarding War Diaries and Intelligence Summaries are contained in F. S. Regs., Part II. and the Staff Manual respectively. Title pages will be prepared in manuscript.

WAR DIARY

or

~~INTELLIGENCE SUMMARY.~~

(Erase heading not required.)

Army Form C. 2118.

For October, 1917.

Place	Date	Hour	Summary of Events and Information	Remarks and references to Appendices
In the Field	Oct/17.		166th. Machine Gun Company.	
	1st		The Company still holding Machine Gun positions in the line.- The whole front up to the present very quiet.	
	3rd.		During the past few days weather very favourable. Little activity.	
	4		Weather conditions changed to that of inclemency, consequently the roads were made very bad, which was a great impediment to both foot and Vehicular traffic. Observation for the past few days very fair.	
	5.		This Company carried out a Programme of Indirect fire, 3,000 rounds being fired.	
	6.		This was repeated, a similar number of rounds being fired,- the chief targets being "Ossus Wood", Honnecourt Wood, and Enemy cross roads.	
	7.		Enemy's Artillery slightly active - the forward areas receiving attention.	
	8.	11-pm	The vicinity of our M.G. position F. 9 was lightly shelled at about this hour. No damage caused.	
	9.	11-pm to 4-10pm	During this period our M.G's carried out a programme of Harassing fire on Honnecourt Wood - 2,500 rounds being fired.	Lieut

A7092 Wt. W12839/M1293 750,000. 1/17. D. D & L., Ltd. Forms/C2118/14.

Army Form C. 2118.

WAR DIARY

or

~~INTELLIGENCE SUMMARY.~~

(Erase heading not required.)

Instructions regarding War Diaries and Intelligence Summaries are contained in F. S. Regs., Part II. and the Staff Manual respectively. Title pages will be prepared in manuscript.

Place	Date	Hour	Summary of Events and Information	Remarks and references to Appendices
In the Field	Oct/17. 10/11	12. midnight.	4 Machine Guns of this Company and 4 Machine Guns of the 196th. Machine Gun Company which constituted a Battery, fired on "Kingston Quarry" 3,000 rounds fired. This shoot was carried out in conjunction with the Artillery. Very little retaliation on the part of the enemy. Enemy Machine Guns firing from the direction of "Canal Wood" and "Honnecourt Wood" concentrated their fire on our M.G. position F. 9.	
			No Casualties to this Company during this period.	
	12.		Enemy Artillery active throughout the day. Between 7-0 p.m. and midnight Enemy artillery paid considerable attention to our forward areas. Intermittent shelling of the Epehy Road during the evening. During our Tour in the line very bad weather prevailed, in consequence visibility was poor. The few spare men kept at Company Headquarters (Parr's Bank) were kept very busy in the construction of a Bath-house and Drying Room, and laying down of trench boards.	[signature] Lieut.
	12/13	night.	The Company was relieved by the 165th. Machine Gun Company and after relief proceeded by march route to Aizecourt-le-Bas and were put under canvas.	
	13.		Company spent the day cleaning Guns, Tripods, Belt boxes etc, and cleaning themselves generally.	
	14/18.		Company commenced a period of training in advanced M.G. work and Company drill. The training being 4 hours per day and time devoted to Games etc after parades. Time was also devoted to Gas drill under Company Gas N.C.O.	

A7092 Wt. W128.9/M1293. 750,000. 1/17. D. D & L., Ltd. Forms/C2118/14.

Instructions regarding War Diaries and Intelligence Summaries are contained in F. S. Regs., Part II. and the Staff Manual respectively. Title pages will be prepared in manuscript.

Army Form C. 2118.

WAR DIARY
or
~~INTELLIGENCE SUMMARY.~~
(Erase heading not required.)

Place	Date	Hour	Summary of Events and Information	Remarks and references to Appendices
In the Field	Oct/17			
	19.	morning.	The whole of the Brigade with Transport was paraded as for Ceremonial and inspected by ~~the~~ Major General WRIGHT, Commanding U.S.A. Forces.	
	20.		Brigade exercise took place in which this Company exercised with Units. After the exercise (during the afternoon) the Company's anti-Gas appliances were inspected by the Company Gas N.C.O.	
	21.	Sunday.	Company attended Church parade at 10-0 a.m.	
	22.		During the morning the Company prepared for the line (packing of Limbers etc.) In the evening the Company, with Transport, moved off by march route and relieved the 165th. Machine Gun Company in the line, - 16 M.G's being in the forward area - 4 M.G's in reserve. 4 of the M.G's in the forward area belonging to the 196th. Machine Gun Company and attached to this Company for Tactical purposes. Company Headquarters taking up Billets in Parr's Bank (Pigeon Ravine).	
	23/26.		Normal activity by Enemy Artillery. Nothing abnormal occurring.	
	27.	3-20 am.	At 3-20 a.m. a concentration Shoot was carried out on Honnecourt Wood and Enemy defences in the vicinity by our Artillery, M.G's and T.M's. At the same time Gas was discharged from 600 Projectors. During this shoot our M.G's fired 7,250 rounds. Little retaliation came from the enemy.	W.R[illegible] Lieut.

A5092. Wt. W12839/M1293. 750,000. 1/17. D. D & L., Ltd. Forms/C2118/14.

Army Form C. 2118.

Instructions regarding War Diaries and Intelligence Summaries are contained in F. S. Regs., Part II. and the Staff Manual respectively. Title pages will be prepared in manuscript.

WAR DIARY
or
~~INTELLIGENCE SUMMARY.~~
(Erase heading not required.)

Place	Date	Hour	Summary of Events and Information	Remarks and references to Appendices
In the Field	Oct/17			
	28/29.		Enemy Artillery very quiet. Observation poor.	
	30/31.		Desultory shelling by Enemy Artillery on our Brigade front. Nothing abnormal happening. Little Aeroplane activity.	
			Company still holding positions in the line.	
			Up to this time Indirect fire by 3 of our M.G's has been carried out nightly.- Average number of rounds fired during night 4,500.	

******************** ... ******************

1st. November, 1917.

for O.C. 166th. Machine Gun Company.
A Rome
Lieut.

D. D. & L., London, E.C.
(A8004) Wt W1771/M2031 750,000 5/17 Sch. 52 Forms/C2118/14

VIII 21
166/55

War Diary

of the

166th M.G. Co

for the period

1st to 30th November

1917

November 1917.

WAR DIARY
or
INTELLIGENCE SUMMARY.
(*Erase heading not required.*)

Army Form C. 2118.

Instructions regarding War Diaries and Intelligence Summaries are contained in F. S. Regs., Part II. and the Staff Manual respectively. Title pages will be prepared in manuscript.

166th Machine Gun Coy.

Place	Date	Hour	Summary of Events and Information	Remarks and references to Appendices
In the Field France. SHEET 57.C S.E. 4	1st.		Company holding Machine Gun positions in the line. Desultory Shelling by the Enemy.	
	4th		During the past few days, visibility poor. the prevailing mists hindering observation considerably. Weather conditions being that of inclemency.	
			Our Machine Guns carrying out a programme of Indirect Fire nightly about 4,500 Rounds being fired each night on selected Enemy defences.	
	7		Again our Machine Guns active on Enemy defences, Tracks & Roads in back areas.	
			Discharge of 800 Gas projectors, fired on C55 d5 (wood) and defences in the vicinity.	
			The Machine Gun Company on our right (165 M.G. Coy) cooperated and 6,000 rounds were expended.	
			Enemy Machine Guns quiet.	
			Activity on our front below normal.	A Rowe Capt.

D. D. & L., London, E.C.
(A8004) Wt W1771/M2031 750,000 5/17 Sch. 52 Forms/C2118/14

November 1917

Instructions regarding War Diaries and Intelligence Summaries are contained in F. S. Regs., Part II. and the Staff Manual respectively. Title pages will be prepared in manuscript.

WAR DIARY
or
INTELLIGENCE SUMMARY.
(Erase heading not required.)

Army Form C. 2118.

16 Machine Gun Coy

Place	Date	Hour	Summary of Events and Information	Remarks and references to Appendices
In the Field.	7/8		There was no hostile activity in retaliation on the Brigade Front	
	8		During the afternoon Enemy shelled HALLHSIE FARM with a heavy calibre shell	
			Enemy Machine Guns fairly quiet.	
	9th		Enemy Artillery active between EPEHY and LEMPIRE and between 9 am to 10 am several 77 mm shells fell in the vicinity top of STORAX AVENUE.	
			Our front line trenches on the left of the Brigade front received some attention from Hostile Artillery	
			During the night 6,000 rounds were expended in Indirect fire on Roads &c behind Enemy's Lines.	
			Enemy Machine Guns fired from the direction of HIGH ST. apparently retaliatory fire.	
	10th 12th		Little activity on the part of the Enemy. Owing to heavy mist, observation was impossible.	[illegible] Capt

D. D. & L., London, E.C.
(A8004) Wt W1771/M2031 750,000 5/17 Sch. 52 Forms/C2118/14

November 1917

Instructions regarding War Diaries and Intelligence Summaries are contained in F. S. Regs., Part II. and the Staff Manual respectively. Title pages will be prepared in manuscript.

WAR DIARY
or
INTELLIGENCE SUMMARY.
(Erase heading not required.)

166th Machine Gun Coy

Army Form C. 2118.

Place	Date	Hour	Summary of Events and Information	Remarks and references to Appendices
In the Field	13.	12.45 am	At this hour under cover of Artillery Barrage and Machine Gun fire a Raiding Party attempted to enter the enemy's post in the N.W. Corner of HONNECOURT WOOD. The Bangalore Torpedoes however failed to explode and the party were unable to effect an entry in the Enemy's wire. Casualties to the Raiding Party being 2 other Ranks - wounded (slightly). Enemy did not retaliate until 1.45 am when our front was lightly shelled. Our Machine Guns fired 15000 Rounds in conjunction with Artillery Barrage at 12.45 am. Throughout the night the Company's Guns were intermittently active on Gaps cut in the Enemy's wire, also during the day against E.A. and on Enemy Communications. Visibility poor owing to heavy mist.	[illegible] Capt

D. D. & L., London, E.C.
(A8604) Wt W1771/M2031 750,000 5/17 Sch. 52 Forms/C2118/14

November 1917

Instructions regarding War Diaries and Intelligence Summaries are contained in F. S. Regs., Part II. and the Staff Manual respectively. Title pages will be prepared in manuscript.

WAR DIARY
or
INTELLIGENCE SUMMARY.
(Erase heading not required.)

Army Form C. 2118.

166th Machine Gun Coy

Place	Date	Hour	Summary of Events and Information	Remarks and references to Appendices
In the Field			Our Machine Guns carried out the usual Indirect Fire programme, firing 5000 Rounds.	[illegible] Capt
		11.45 am	A burst of 20 Rounds was fired at a [illegible] plane, further firing was impossible owing to heavy mist. The aeroplane had evidently lost direction.	
			Enemy Machine Gun active on our Tracks after 4pm when mist became very thick.	
	14th		Several [illegible] [illegible] ST. during the night & the Machine Gun in the S.W. corner of HAVRINCOURT WOOD was also active.	
	15.		Situation normal, Observation was again hampered by mist.	
	16/18		Activity that of normal, on both sides.	
	19th/20		In the evening and during the early hours of the morning, moves were carried out by Gun Teams in Reserve at LIMERICK POST to Battery positions in BANTAM TRACK, likewise the guns of this Company	

D. D. & L., London, E.C. (A8004) Wt W1771/M2031 750,000 5/17 Sch. 52 Forms/C2118/14

November 1917.

Instructions regarding War Diaries and Intelligence Summaries are contained in F. S. Regs., Part II. and the Staff Manual respectively. Title pages will be prepared in manuscript.

WAR DIARY
or
INTELLIGENCE SUMMARY.
(Erase heading not required.)

Army Form C. 2118.

166th Machine Gun Coy

Place	Date	Hour	Summary of Events and Information	Remarks and references to Appendices
In the Field	19th		in M G emplacements on the left of Brigade Front moved to Battery positions in DENNING AVENUE.	[signature] Capt
		10pm	Company Hd. Qrs was established at Brigade H.Q. for operations. Present Coy Hd. Qrs being known as Advanced Coy Hd Qrs. 3 Machine Gun Batteries were organised & called by TONE, BANTAM and HIGH DENNING. The first 2 coming under the Command of 164 Inf. Bde and the latter under 235 M.G. Coy Group Commander.	
	20.	6.20 am	At this hour under cover of Artillery Trench Mortar & Machine Gun Barrages an Attack was launched by the 165 Infantry Brigade on our Right. In conjunction with the above operation a Dummy Tank and figures were put out from the BIRDCAGE which drew much of the Enemy's fire. Our Machine Guns placed Barrages on selected positions in the Enemy's line. a total of Rounds being fired during the day. Also Rounds were fired when S.O.S. calls were sent up. At Zero hour 1320 Gas projectors were	

D. D. & L., London, E.C. (A8204) Wt W1771/M2031 750,000 5/17 Sch. 52 Forms/C2118/14

November 1917

WAR DIARY
or
INTELLIGENCE SUMMARY.
(Erase heading not required.)

Army Form C. 2118.

166th Machine Gun Coy

Instructions regarding War Diaries and Intelligence Summaries are contained in F. S. Regs., Part II. and the Staff Manual respectively. Title pages will be prepared in manuscript.

Place	Date	Hour	Summary of Events and Information	Remarks and references to Appendices
In the Field			satisfactorily discharged against LES TRANNES and CANAL WOOD in our direction.	
		4.30 pm	At this hour a Barrage from our Artillery, Trench Mortars and Machine Guns was placed upon selected points of the Enemy line opposite to Right Brigade.	
	20/21		During the night the situation on the Brigade's front = Normal	
			A total of 10.000 Rounds was fired from Battns STONE, BANTAM and DENNING.	
	21		These Barrage positions with the exception of NEAR DENNING were vacated by 5 pm and the original M G positions in the left Brigade Sector were manned as prior to the attack. During these operations the company suffered no casualties.	
	21/22		During the night Hostile Machine Guns fired occasional bursts, bullets falling to the Right of F 11. M G position. Guns R 26 and R 27 fired a total of 3400 Rounds (Indirect Fire) into the SW corner of BANTEUX RAVINE at	[illegible]

D. D. & L., London, E.C.
(A8004) Wt W1771/M2031 750,000 5/17 Sch. 52 Forms/C2118/14

November 1917

Instructions regarding War Diaries and Intelligence Summaries are contained in F. S. Regs., Part II. and the Staff Manual respectively. Title pages will be prepared in manuscript.

WAR DIARY
or
INTELLIGENCE SUMMARY.
(Erase heading not required.)

Army Form C. 2118.

166th Machine Gun Coy

Place	Date	Hour	Summary of Events and Information	Remarks and references to Appendices
In the Field			R 36. a. 80.10. The DENNING BATTERY (Guns 3 & 4) fired a total of 5,000 rounds throughout the night on to BRIDGE at N. 25. d. 85.65 from orders received from 235 M.G. Coy. Remainder of our Brigade front - activity normal.	
	22		Our aeroplanes active during the morning.	
		2.30pm	A few shells fell round KILDARE POST otherwise little hostile activity.	
			During the night our Machine Guns fired a total of 12,250 rounds on Enemy Defences around the Village of Honnecourt & neighbourhood of ST QUENTIN CANAL. Activity on the part of the enemy noticed to have increased slightly.	[illegible] Capt
	23		Enemy active with his Artillery, the Road EPEHY - VILLERS GUISLAIN receiving a fair amount of attention. Observation proved only ~~bad~~ fair.	
		4.30pm	Our Machine Guns carrying out harassing fire on the enemies defences in the region of Honnecourt	

D. D. & L., London, E.C. (A8041) Wt. W1771/M2031 750,000 5/17 Sch. 52 Forms/C2118/14

November 1917

Army Form C. 2118.

Instructions regarding War Diaries and Intelligence Summaries are contained in F. S. Regs., Part II. and the Staff Manual respectively. Title pages will be prepared in manuscript.

WAR DIARY
or
INTELLIGENCE SUMMARY.
(Erase heading not required.)

16th Machine Gun Coy

Place	Date	Hour	Summary of Events and Information	Remarks and references to Appendices
In the Field.	24		During the day Our Machine Guns co-operated with the Brigade on our left. At 5.45 am 3500 rounds were fired on point M.25.d.2.2. and on S.O.S. Lines during the night 10.250 rounds, and 15.800 Rds were expended on Indirect Fire on Road, Tracks & Enemy Defences. In all 33,500 rounds were expended.	
	25.		The Machine Guns situate on the Left of the Brigade front, carried out Indirect Fire during the night and also assisted the Brigade on our left during their attack at 7 am on 25/11/17. A total of 15.800 rounds being fired.	
			During the day visibility was poor.	
	26.		Little Hostile Activity on our front. Observation was not good. Much wind & towards night Rain. Snow commencing to fall about 11.30 pm.	
	27		Activity on Both Sides normal. Observation fair, weather boisterous. Indirect fire.	
	28		Our Machine Guns carried out usual [illegible] 7,500 rounds being expended. Abnormal movement on the part of the Enemy observed in the region of Honnecourt	

[illegible]

D. D. & L., London, E.C.
(A8004) Wt W1771/M2031 750,000 5/17 Sch. 52 Forms/C2118/14

November 1917

Instructions regarding War Diaries and Intelligence Summaries are contained in F. S. Regs., Part II. and the Staff Manual respectively. Title pages will be prepared in manuscript.

WAR DIARY
or
INTELLIGENCE SUMMARY.
(Erase heading not required.)

Army Form C. 2118.

166th Machine Gun Coy

Place	Date	Hour	Summary of Events and Information	Remarks and references to Appendices
In the field.	28/29		Throughout the night our Machine Guns very active on Enemy approaches to Honnecourt wood & Banteux Ravine also on BRIDGES over the CANAL in the vicinity.	[illegible] Capt
	29.		Enemy Artillery more active than usual. VILLERS-GUISLAIN receiving considerable attention from new H.V. gun from direction of HONNECOURT. Observation fairly good	
	30.	6.45	At this hour Enemy opened out with his Artillery & Trench Mortars, bombarding heavily our front line & supports, on this Brigade front and the Brigade on our Left. Our Machine Guns immediately opened fire on their S.O.S. Lines. After a short time the enemy was observed to have penetrated our line. His chief concentration appeared to be along the Valley N.E of VILLERS GUISLAIN, the low lying ground in the vicinity of HONNECOURT WOOD and again in the vicinity of PIGEON QUARRY. In the former place he came through our lines and advanced in a S.W. direction in very large numbers. He also congregated in and around PIGEON QUARRY in mass from whence he made his way Westwards. Owing to ~~heavy~~ mist observation was rather bad.	

D. D. & L., London, E.C. (A8004) Wt W1771/M2631 750,000 5/17 Sch. 52 Forms/C2118/14

November 1917

Instructions regarding War Diaries and Intelligence Summaries are contained in F. S. Regs., Part II. and the Staff Manual respectively. Title pages will be prepared in manuscript.

WAR DIARY
or
INTELLIGENCE SUMMARY.
(Erase heading not required.)

Army Form C. 2118.

166th Machine Gun Coy.

Place	Date	Hour	Summary of Events and Information	Remarks and references to Appendices
In the Field	30		Many of our Machine Guns brought direct fire to bear on the enemy at a close range, causing him heavy casualties. During this period hostile aeroplanes were exceedingly active and several casualties were suffered by our Machine Gun Teams through enemy aircraft flying low and firing upon them.	
			2 Additional Machine Guns at Coy. Hd. Qrs. PARRS BANK were brought into action firing a number of belts from positions in the open with good effect.	
		8.30	About this time enemy progressed very slowly. All Machine Guns Teams suffered casualties from well directed & organised rifle fire. There is no information available regarding the fate of 7 guns & teams. Seven guns were put out of action including one shot by enemy aeroplane and one struck by enemy bomb. The majority however were rendered "Hors-de-Combat" by direct sniping on the part of the enemy. 2 Guns were brought out of action. The action throughout was conspicuous for the manner in which enemy infantry used their rifles against Machine Guns and for the valiant attempt made by	

D. D. & L., London, E.C. (A8604) Wt W1771/M2031 750,000 5/17 Sch. 52 Forms/C2118/14

November 1917 — **War Diary** (continued). — 166 Machine Gun Coy.

Place	Date	Hour	Summary of Events and Information
Infre Field	30.		by our men to recover and bring out their guns, although badly damaged. In one case no less than 5 men in succession being hit in a vain attempt to recover a damaged gun.
			4 Guns composing a Battery in X.21.d.2.2 fought an effective & well carried out action after the enemy had broken through and their S.O.S. fire was no longer effective. These guns were frequently moved from one position to another to meet the onslaught of the enemy at close ranges and were in action for about 7¾ hours during which time they fired approximately 50.000 rounds.
		2.pm.	Divisional Troops & Demonstration platoons were brought up from the back areas & dug a Trench in X road crossing 14 WILLOWS ROAD. Later during the day M.G. Coy of the 16th Brigade came up 8 guns of this company being placed under the command of O.C. 166 M.G. Coy.
			The Company suffered a total of 4 Officers & 77 other Ranks Casualties.

30/11/17

[illegible] Captain.
O.C. 166. M.G. Coy

166/55 Vol 22

War Diary

of the

166th Machine Gun Coy.

for the period

1st to 31st December 1917

December 1917.

Instructions regarding War Diaries and Intelligence Summaries are contained in F. S. Regs., Part II. and the Staff Manual respectively. Title pages will be prepared in manuscript.

DIARY ~~or INTELLIGENCE SUMMARY.~~

(Erase heading not required.)

166th Machine [Gun Company]

Place	Date	Hour	Summary of Events and Information	Remarks and references to Appendices
In the field EPEHY	1/3rd		Company was relieved in the line by 110 M.G. Coy. and proceeded to Tincourt. Here Company rested 2 days prior to proceeding to Divisional Area PERONNE. After staying here two days entrained for	
	9		AUBIGNY thence by March Route to IZEL-LES-HAMEAU. 2 days were spent here.	
	11.		Company left IZEL-LES-HAMEAU and marched a distance of about 7 miles to the village of TINCQUETTE	
	12		The following day continued March Route through the village of BAILEUL, MARQUAY, BRYAS, OSTREVILLE, HEUCHIN to HESTRUS. Resting here over night & proceeded next day a distance of about 6 Kilos passing through EPS. PETIT-ANVIN. BERGANEUSE- to EQUIRRE again spending the night in the last named village.	R. [signature] Lieut for Captain
	14		Move from this village was commenced at 9.30 am by March Route to present Area. - PETIGNY	(Map BOMY Ref. R.32.a.)

A.5092 Wt. W12839/M1293 750,000. 1/17. D. D & L., Ltd. Forms/C2118/14.

December 1917

Instructions regarding War Diaries and Intelligence Summaries are contained in F. S. Regs., Part II. and the Staff Manual respectively. Title pages will be prepared in manuscript.

WAR DIARY
or
INTELLIGENCE SUMMARY.
(Erase heading not required.)

166 Machine Gun Coy

Army Form C. 2118.

Place	Date	Hour	Summary of Events and Information	Remarks and references to Appendices
In the Field			At this place company was billeted and provisions for the re-organisation of the Company being made	
	1/31		Company and Transport carried out Ordinary duties of the Machine Gun Company as far as personnel would permit.	
			During this period of rest, Estaminet in the village of PETIGNY were opened for the Company for the sale of Coffee etc all day, & as Reading & Writing Rooms.	
			Construction of a Harness Room commenced & general improvement of Company's billets.	
	25		Christmas Day, Company attended Divine Service with Unit of the Brigade at ERNY - ST - JULIEN	
	31.		Company continued training which included firing on Range. Gas Drill under Company Gas N.C.O.	Lieut for Captain 166th M.G. Coy.

War Diary Vol 23

of the

166th M. G. Coy.

for the period

1st to 31st January

1918.

January 1918

Instructions regarding War Diaries and Intelligence Summaries are contained in F. S. Regs., Part II. and the Staff Manual respectively. Title Pages will be prepared in manuscript.

WAR DIARY
or
INTELLIGENCE SUMMARY

(Erase heading not required.)

Army Form C. 2118.

166 Machine Gun Coy

H.Q. 166th INFANTRY BDE. No. ... Date 4.2.18

Place	Date	Hour	Summary of Events and Information	Remarks and references to Appendices
			Ref Map: BOMY	
PETIGNY			During the month Company carried out Training in Machine Gun Drill, Advanced Drill, Guard mounting, Action from Limbers, MG firing on Range, Tactical Exercise, etc. etc. Gas Mask Drill being carried out in conjunction with above.	[illegible] Capt
			The weather during the fore part of the month was inclement and out of door training was impeded. Lectures on Anti-Aircraft Sights, Clinometers, Elevating & Traversing Dial, Luminous Sights etc. etc. were given.	
			Football matches were played on Wednesdays & Saturdays of each week, with the various Units in the Brigade.	
	1st		Company marched to ERNY-ST-JULIEN for Brigade Divine Service.	
	4th		Company proceeded to AINTREE RACECOURSE for Demonstration with Units of the Brigade. Tea being served up on the parade ground. On return Company had dinner about 4 pm.	

2449 Wt. W14957/M90 750,000 1/16 J.B.C. & A. Forms/C.2118/12.

January 1918

Army Form C. 2118.

Instructions regarding War Diaries and Intelligence Summaries are contained in F. S. Regs., Part II. and the Staff Manual respectively. Title Pages will be prepared in manuscript.

WAR DIARY
or
~~INTELLIGENCE SUMMARY~~

(Erase heading not required.)

166th Machine Gun Coy

Place	Date	Hour	Summary of Events and Information	Remarks and references to Appendices
			Ref map. BOMY	
PETIGNY	8	12 noon	Lecture in Billets by Brigadier General Kentish	
	9		Brigade Concert party gave a concert in the village of PETIGNY for this Company	
	11		Lecture to all Officers and NCOs by the DMGO	
	13	11.0	Church Service parade for the Brigade at ERNY - ST. JULIEN	
	21	2pm	Officers & NCOs of this Company proceeded to rendezvous for Tactical Exercise under ~~the~~ B.G.C. One M.G and Gun Teams of this Company also being employed for this Exercise	
	25		Action from Limbers practiced by 4 Sections & Transport. The Company proceeded to the Classification Range X 30 b 5.5 for this action	
	29		Company paraded with Limbers & proceeded to the parade ground in R 29 a for Inspection by the Corps Commander, after which the B.G.C. presented the "1914 Star" ribands to Officers NCOs & men of the Unit in the Brigade. 1 Officer & 6 other Ranks being the recipients in this Company	

[signature] Capt.

January 1918

WAR DIARY
or
~~INTELLIGENCE~~ SUMMARY
(Erase heading not required.)

166 Machine Gun Coy.

Army Form C. 2118.

Instructions regarding War Diaries and Intelligence Summaries are contained in F. S. Regs., Part II. and the Staff Manual respectively. Title Pages will be prepared in manuscript.

Place	Date	Hour	Summary of Events and Information	Remarks and references to Appendices
			Ref. Map. BOMY	
PETIGNY	29	6.15	The Brigade Concert Party gave a concert in the village of PETIGNY for the Company	
	30		Company paraded with Limbers and proceeded to the Range at BRICK WORKS near ERNY-ST JULIEN where the Company had an Inter Sector Competition of "Action from Limbers against Time".	
	31		Company proceeded by Route March to X 25.d.6.6 to witness the Divisional Wiring Competition which was won by the 1/7 King's L'pool R. (165 Bde)	
		6 pm	Night operations in Marking out Barrage positions	

A. [illegible] Rowe Captain
OC 166 M.G. Coy

2449 Wt. W14957/M90 750,000 1/16 J.B.C. & A. Forms/C.2118/12.

VR 24

War Diary

of the

166th M. G. Coy

for the period

1st to 28th Febry.

1918

February 1918 — 166 Machine Gun Coy

Army Form C. 2118.

Instructions regarding War Diaries and Intelligence Summaries are contained in F. S. Regs., Part II. and the Staff Manual respectively. Title pages will be prepared in manuscript.

WAR DIARY
or
~~INTELLIGENCE SUMMARY.~~
(Erase heading not required.)

Place	Date	Hour	Summary of Events and Information (Ref. Map BOMY)	Remarks and references to Appendices
PETIGNY	1st/9th		Company completing programme of Training and the carrying out of Tactical Exercises etc etc	
	11	9.30	Company moved from Billets in PETIGNY (Bomy area) and proceeded with Transport by March Route to the village of PIPPEMONT (1/50,000 Hesdin Reserve Area) here the Company rested over night & proceeded the next day to the village of CHOCQUES. Ref Map FRANCE (Sh. 36B D 5 b) Four days (inclusive) were spent here during which time practice in Immediate Action & Gun Drill was carried out also firing on short range with M.Gs	
	14		Company moved to ESSARS. (in Divisional Reserve) During the Company's stay at this place (viz) 12 days, Company Drill, Gas Drill Arm Drill & Machine Gun Drill being carried out, special attention being paid to Gas Drill. Falling in on Company Alarm Post practised in case	[illegible signature]

D. D. & L., London, E.C. (A7883) Wt W809/M1672 350,000 4/17 Sch. 52a Forms/C/2118/14

February 1917 | WAR DIARY or ~~INTELLIGENCE~~ SUMMARY. (Erase heading not required.) | 166th Machine Gun Coy | Army Form C. 2118.

Instructions regarding War Diaries and Intelligence Summaries are contained in F. S. Regs., Part II. and the Staff Manual respectively. Title pages will be prepared in manuscript.

Place	Date	Hour	Summary of Events and Information (Ref map. GORRE)	Remarks and references to Appendices
In the Field			of an event arising which necessitated the closing up of Troops.	
			While the Company was in Divisional Reserve Officers & Senior N.C.Os of the Company made daily reconnaisance of the line.	
	24	830.	The Company received Orders to move at once to GORRE and were billeted in this village for 2 nights pending a move to relieve the 165 M.G. Coy	
	27.	930.	Company moved up into the Line relieving the 165th Machine Gun Coy in the Left Brigade Sector.	
	28.		Coy Hd Qrs being situate in LE PLANTIN (A.3.c ref map GORRE) Village Line. The Transport Section moving to Transport Lines in the Chateau Grounds GORRE	
			During this period in the line Activity was Normal.	

[illegible] Captain
O.C 166 M.G. Coy

www.ingramcontent.com/pod-product-compliance
Lightning Source LLC
Chambersburg PA
CBHW081437160426
43193CB00013B/2307